Ceramic Smoker Cookbook

Ultimate Smoker Cookbook for Real Pitmasters, Irresistible Recipes for Your Ceramic Smoker

Adam Jones

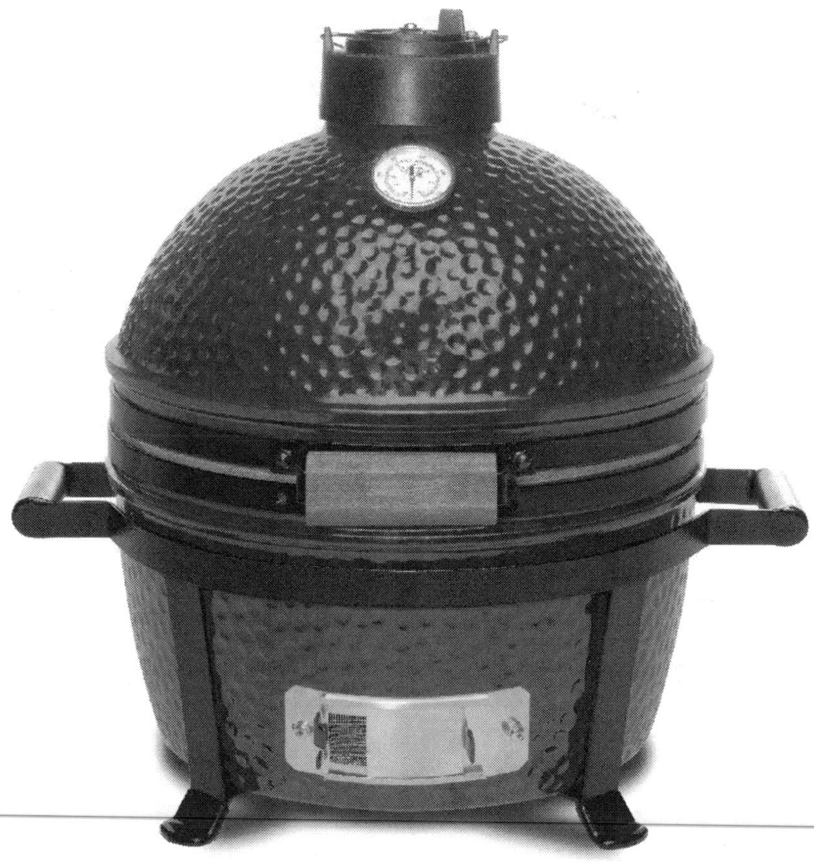

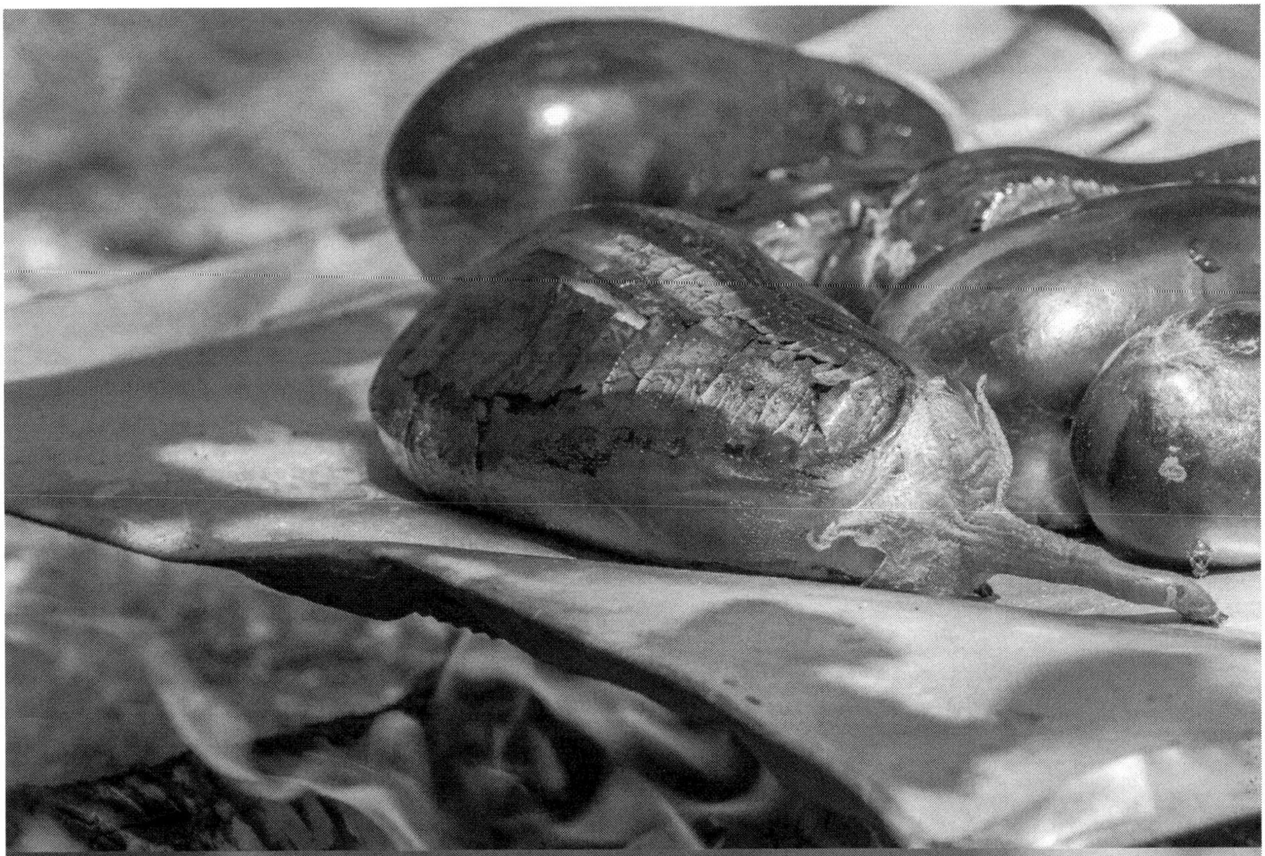

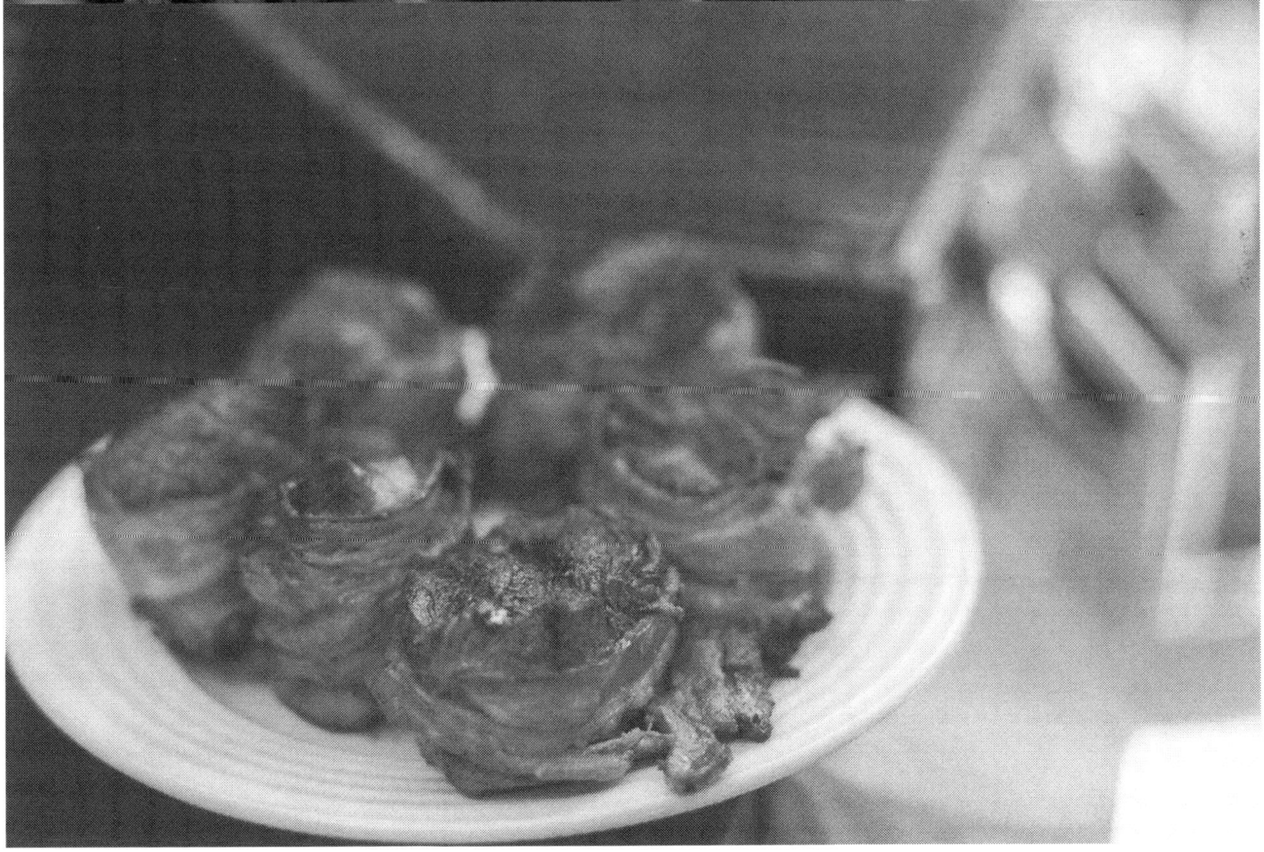

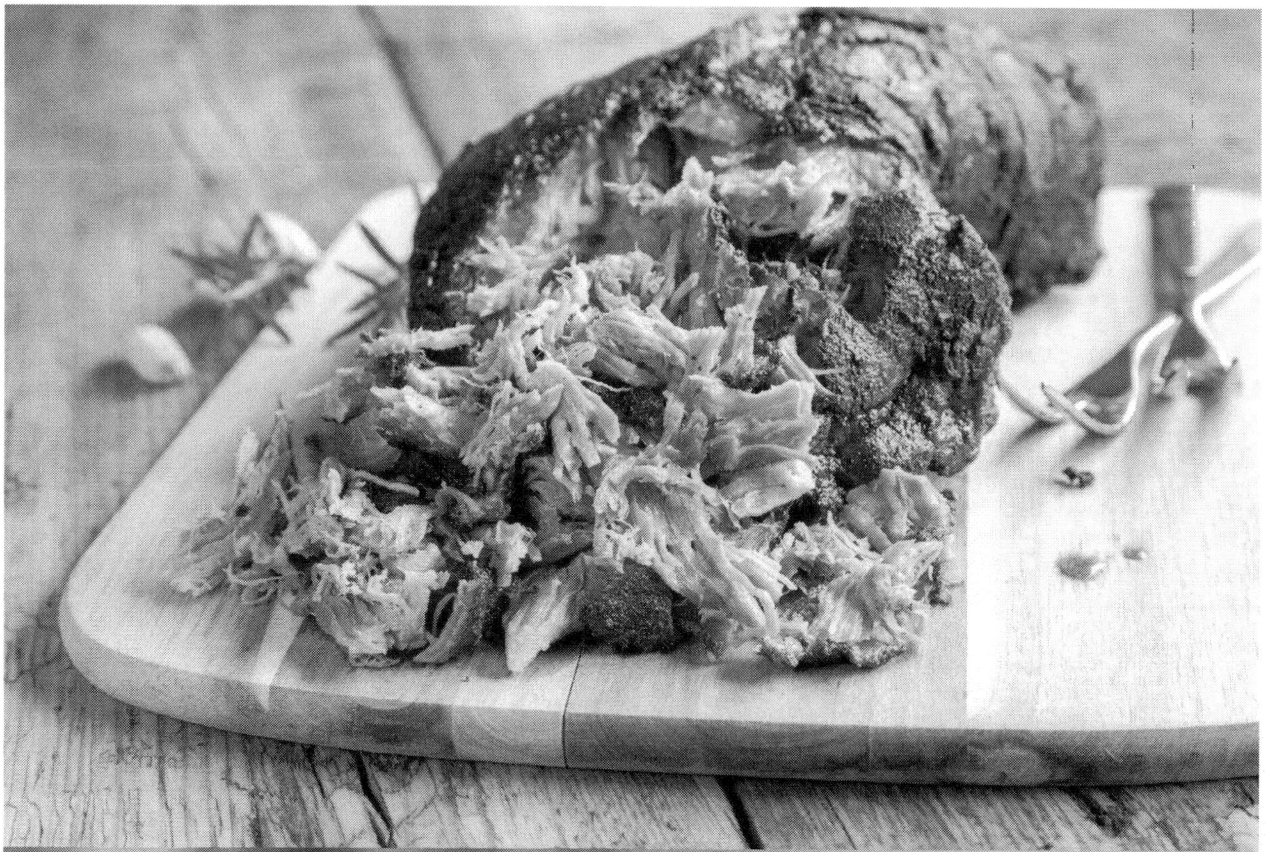

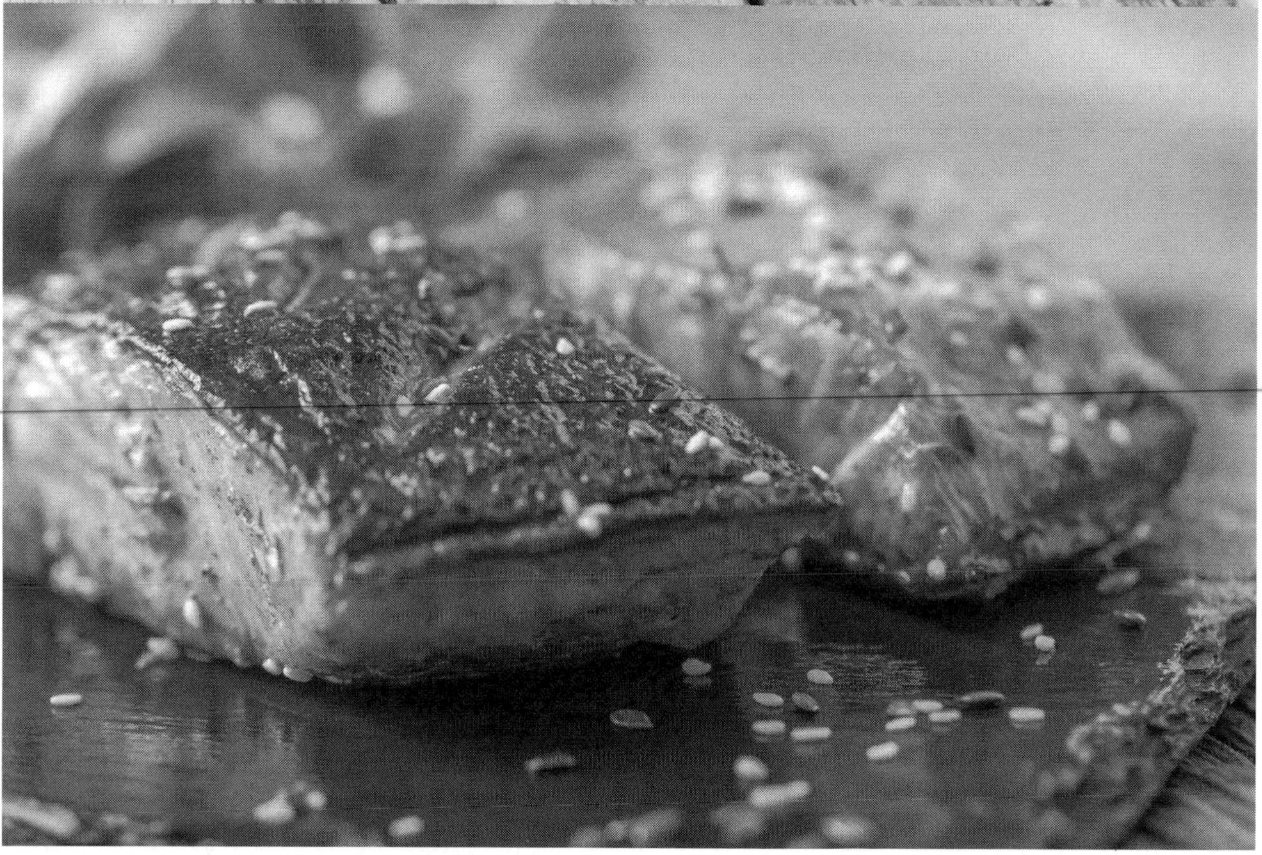

TABLE OF CONTENTS

Introduction 8

BEEF 9

Sweet Apple Smoked Beef Ribs 9
Hot Smoked Beef Brisket Oregano 12
Cheesy Smoked Flank Steak Roll 15
Smoked Beef Tenderloin in Bacon Wrap 18
Smoked Corned Beef 20

PORK 22

Spicy Smoked Pork Butt Black Pepper 22
Smoked Pork Ribs with Apple Aroma 25
Hickory Sweet Honey Smoked Pulled Pork 28
Smoked Pork Belly with Black Sauce 31
Peach Glazed Smoked Pork Loin 34

LAMB 36

Smoked Lemon Lamb Leg Marjoram 36
....36
Smoked Lamb Ribs with Apricot Glaze 38
Milky Smoked Lamb Chops with White Sauce 41
Cheesy Smoked Lamb Roast with Orange Marinade 44
Spiced Smoked Lamb Tender 46

FISH **49**

Lemon Rosemary Smoked Sardines 49
Buttery Smoked Salmon Black Pepper 51
Lemon Smoked Red Snapper with Fresh Dill and Rosemary 53
Citrus Smoked Kipper with Soy Sauce 55

SEAFOOD **57**

Smoked Shrimp Skewer Curry 57
Smoked Scallop Chili 59
Gingery Smoked Oyster Alder 61
Lemon Smoked Mussel Rosemary 63

VEGETABLES **65**

Smoked Eggplant Paprika with Oregano 65
Smoked Red Tomato Garlic 67
Bacon Stuffed Smoked Cabbage 69
Juicy Smoked Onion with Whiskey Glaze 71

CHICKEN **73**

Smoked Chicken Breast with Strawberry Glaze 73
Spicy Smoked Chicken Wings 75
Savory Smoked Chicken Crispy 77

TURKEY **79**

Chili Tomato Smoked Turkey Fritter 79
Onion Apple Smoked Whole Turkey 81
Smoked Juicy Turkey Drumsticks 83

GAME 85

Smoked Venison in Bacon Blanket 85
Smoked Cornish Hen with Apple Coating 87
Smoked Quails Jalapeno 89
Savory Smoked Pheasant 91

Information About Smoking Meat 93

What is the primary difference between Barbecuing a meat and Smoking it? 93
The core difference between cold and hot smoking 94
The different types of available Smokers 95
The different styles of smokers 96
The different types of wood and their benefits 97
The different types of Charcoal 99
The basic preparations 100
The core elements of smoking! 101

Conclusion 102

Get Your FREE Gift 103

Other books by Adam Jones 104

INTRODUCTION

Smoking meat or making BBQ is not only a means of cooking but for some individuals and classy enthusiasts, this is a form of Art! Or dare I say a form of lifestyle! Enthusiasts all around the world have been experimenting and dissecting the secrets of perfectly smoked meat for decades now, and in our golden age, perhaps they have cracked it up completely!In our age, the technique of Barbecuing or Smoking meat has been perfected to such a level, that a BBQ Grill is pretty much an essential amenity found in all backyard or sea-beach parties!

This is the drinking fountain for the more hip and adventurous people, who prefer to have a nice chat with their friends and families while smoking up a few batches of Burger Patty for them to enjoy. But here's the thing, while this art might seem as a very easy form of cooking which only requires you to flip meats over and over! Mastering it might be a little bit difficult if you don't know have the proper information with you.And that is exactly why I have written this chapter, where I will walk you through the very basic elements of Smoking, so that you may start off experimenting with the recipes in no time at all!Let's start with a very basic question, the answer to which should be known to all budding smokers and master pitters out there!

<u>FIND MORE INFORMATION ABOUT SMOKING MEAT AT THE END OF THE BOOK</u>

BEEF
Sweet Apple Smoked Beef Ribs

(TOTAL COOK TIME 5 HOURS 10 MINUTES)

INGREDIENTS FOR 10 SERVINGS

- Beef ribs (5-lbs., 2.3-kgs)

THE RUB

- White sugar – ½ cup
- Brown sugar – ½ cup
- Salt – 2 tablespoons

- Black pepper – 1 teaspoon
- Paprika – 1 tablespoon
- Garlic powder – 2 teaspoons

THE GLAZE

- Apple juice – 1 cup

THE FIRE

- Preheat a smoker an hour prior to smoking.
- Use charcoal Apple woods for smoking.
- Soak the Apple wood chips for about an hour before using

METHOD

1. Cut and trim the excess fats from the rubs then place set aside.
2. Combine the rub ingredients—white sugar. Brown sugar, salt, black pepper, paprika, and garlic in a bowl then mix well.
3. Rub the beef ribs with the spice mixture then let it sit while you are preparing the ceramic smoker.
4. Prepare a ceramic smoker for indirect heat and preheat to 225°F (107°C). Use charcoal and soaked apple wood chips for smoking.
5. Set the rack and place the ceramic plate and grate on it.
6. Once the ceramic smoker has reached the desired temperature, place the seasoned beef ribs on the grate and smoke the beef ribs for 2 hours. Use the vent to control the temperature.
7. After the first 2 hours of smoking, open the ceramic smoker and take the beef ribs out of the smoker.
8. Place the beef ribs in a disposable aluminum pan then baste apple juice all over the beef ribs. Drizzle the remaining apple juice over the beef ribs.
9. Cover the disposable aluminum pan with aluminum foil then return it back to the ceramic smoker.
10. Maintain the temperature of the ceramic smoker at 225°F (107°C) and smoke the beef ribs for another 2 hours.

11. After the second 2 hours, open the lid and remove the aluminum pan from the smoker.

12. Carefully remove the aluminum foil and return the beef ribs once again to the ceramic smoker directly on the grate.

13. Smoke the beef ribs for an hour or until the internal temperature has reached 180°F (82°C).

14. Once it is done, remove the smoked beef ribs from the ceramic smoker then let it sit for about 10 minutes.

15. Cut the smoked beef ribs into slices then serve.

16. Enjoy!

Hot Smoked Beef Brisket Oregano

(Total cook time 5 hours 10 minutes)

Ingredients for 10 servings

- Beef brisket (6-lbs., 2.7-kgs)

The Rub

- Olive oil – ¼ cup
- Dried rosemary – 1 tablespoon
- Garlic powder – 2 tablespoons
- Brown sugar – 2 tablespoons
- Paprika – 2 ½ tablespoons

- Cayenne pepper – 2 ½ tablespoons
- Oregano – 1 ½ tablespoons
- Thyme – 1 tablespoon
- Salt – 2 ¼ tablespoons
- Black pepper – 1 tablespoon

The Glaze

- Apple cider vinegar – 1 cup

The Fire

- Preheat a smoker an hour prior to smoking.
- Use charcoal Hickory woods for smoking.
- Soak the Hickory wood chips for about an hour before using

Method

1. Place dried rosemary, garlic powder, brown sugar, paprika, cayenne pepper, oregano, thyme, salt, and black pepper in a bowl.
2. Pour olive oil over the spice then stir until combined.
3. Trim the excess fats from the brisket than rub with the spice mixture.
4. Tightly cover the beef brisket with plastic wrap then store in the fridge for at least 3 hours. If you have time, you can marinate it overnight.
5. Place charcoal and soaked Hickory wood chips in a ceramic smoker.
6. Light a fire in the ceramic smoker then preheat it to 250°F (121°C).
7. Set the rack in the ceramic smoker then insert a ceramic plate and grated in the ceramic smoker.
8. Place a water pan on the ceramic plate then wait until the ceramic smoker has reached the desired temperature.
9. Once the smoker is ready, remove the beef brisket from the refrigerator then unwrap it and directly put it on the smoker with the fat side down.
10. Smoke the beef brisket 12 hours—2 hours per pound, and spray with apple cider vinegar once every 2 hours. Use the vent to control the temperature.

11. Once the internal temperature has reached 180°F (82°C), remove the smoked beef brisket from the smoker.

12. Quickly wrap the smoked beef brisket with aluminum foil then let it sit for about an hour.

13. Unwrap the smoked beef brisket then cut into slices.

14. Serve and enjoy.

Cheesy Smoked Flank Steak Roll

(total cook time 5 hours 10 minutes)

Ingredients for 10 servings

- Flank steak (2-lbs., 0.9-kgs)

THE RUB

- Salt – ½ teaspoon
- Pepper – ½ teaspoon

THE FILLING

- Butter – 1 tablespoon
- Chopped onion – ¼ cup
- Minced garlic – 2 teaspoons
- Chopped bell pepper – ¼ cup
- Crumbled blue cheese – ¾ cup

THE GLAZE

- Olive oil – 2 tablespoons

THE FIRE

- Preheat a smoker an hour prior to smoking.
- Use charcoal Oak woods for smoking.
- Soak the Oak wood chips for about an hour before using

METHOD

1. Preheat a saucepan over medium heat then melt butter in it.
2. Once the butter is melted, stir in chopped onion and minced garlic then sauté until wilted and aromatic.
3. Remove the sautéed onion and garlic from heat then let it cool.
4. Cut the flank steak into thin large sheet then place on a flat surface.
5. Spread the sautéed onion and garlic on the flank steak then sprinkle chopped bell pepper and crumbled blue cheese on top.
6. Roll the flank steak then set aside.
7. Light a fire in a ceramic smoker with charcoal and soaked Oak wood chips.

8. Set the rack in the ceramic smoker then place a ceramic plate and a grate on it.

9. Preheat the ceramic smoker to 400°F (204°C) and wait until it reaches the desired temperature.

10. Once the smoker has reached the desired temperature, place the flank steak roll directly on the grate.

11. Smoke the flank steak roll for 4 hours or until the internal temperature has reached 145°F (63°C).

12. Remove the smoked flank steak roll from the ceramic smoker then place on a flat surface. Let it cool.

13. Cut the smoked flank steak roll into slices then arrange on a serving dish.

14. Serve and enjoy.

Smoked Beef Tenderloin in Bacon Wrap

(Total cook time 3 hours 15 minutes)

Ingredients for 10 servings

- Beef tenderloin (1.5-lbs., 0.7-kgs)
- Bacon – 10 slices

THE SPICE

- Olive oil – 3 tablespoons
- Salt – 1 teaspoon
- Pepper – ¾ teaspoon

THE FIRE

- Preheat a smoker an hour prior to smoking.
- Use charcoal Mesquite woods for smoking.
- Soak the Mesquite wood chips for about an hour before using

METHOD

1. Cut the bacon slices into halves then set aside.
2. Cut the beef tenderloin into 2 inches thick then wrap each loin with bacon.
3. Place charcoal and soaked Mesquite wood chips in a ceramic smoker then light a fire in it.
4. Preheat the ceramic smoker to 300°F (148°C) and set the rack in it. Insert a ceramic plate and a grate in the ceramic smoker.
5. Once the ceramic smoker has reached the desired temperature, arrange the bacon wrapped loin directly on the grate then drizzle olive oil over the wrapped loin.
6. Sprinkle salt and pepper on top then smoke the wrapped loin for an hour.
7. Flip the wrapped loin then smoke for another hour.
8. Once it is done, remove the smoked wrapped loin from the ceramic smoker then arrange on a serving dish.
9. Serve and enjoy.

SMOKED CORNED BEEF

(TOTAL COOK TIME 5 HOURS 20 MINUTES)

INGREDIENTS FOR 10 SERVINGS

- Corned beef brisket (4-lbs., 1.8-kgs)

THE RUB

- Black pepper – ¼ cup
- Brown sugar – ½ cup
- Garlic powder – 3 tablespoons
- Coriander – 3 tablespoons
- Mustard – 2 tablespoons
- Onion powder – 2 tablespoons

THE WATER BATH

- Beef broth – 2 cups

THE FIRE

- Preheat a smoker an hour prior to smoking.
- Use charcoal Hickory woods for smoking.
- Soak the Hickory wood chips for about an hour before using

METHOD

1. Season the corned beef brisket with black pepper, brown sugar, garlic powder, coriander, mustard, and onion powder.
2. Wrap the corned beef with plastic wrap and let it sit for at least an hour.
3. Place charcoal and soaked Hickory wood chips in a ceramic smoker then light a fire in it.
4. Preheat the ceramic smoker to 275°F (135°C) and set the rack in the ceramic smoker. Insert a ceramic plate and a grate in it.
5. Once the smoker is ready, unwrap the seasoned corned beef and place directly on the grate.
6. Smoke the seasoned corned beef for 3 hours or until the internal temperature has reached 165°F (74°C).
7. Once the corned beef has reached the desired internal temperature, insert a water pan with beef broth and place on the ceramic place.
8. Continue smoking the corned beef for 2 hours or until the internal temperature of the smoked corned beef has reached 200°F (93°C).
9. Remove the smoked corned beef from the smoker and transfer to a cutting board. Let it sit for 20 minutes.
10. Cut the smoked corned into slices then serve.

PORK

Spicy Smoked Pork Butt Black Pepper

(TOTAL COOK TIME 6 HOURS 10 MINUTES)

Ingredients for 10 servings

- Pork Butt (6-lbs., 2.7-kgs)

The Injection

- Apple juice – ¾ cup
- Water – 6 tablespoons
- Worcestershire sauce – ¾ tablespoon
- Salt – ¾ tablespoon

- Sugar – ¾ tablespoon

The Marinade

- Chopped onion – 6 tablespoons
- Water – 3 tablespoons
- Worcestershire sauce – 3 tablespoons
- Minced garlic – 3 tablespoons
- Soy sauce – 1 ½ tablespoons

The Rub

- Brown sugar – 6 tablespoons
- Sweet paprika – 6 tablespoons
- Salt – 3 tablespoons
- Chili powder – 3 tablespoons
- Mustard – 3 tablespoons
- Black pepper – ¾ tablespoons
- Ginger – ½ teaspoon

The Glaze

- Apple juice – ¾ cup
- Water – ¾ cup
- Cider vinegar – 3 tablespoons

The Fire

- Preheat a smoker an hour prior to smoking.
- Use charcoal Cherry woods for smoking.
- Soak the Cherry wood chips for about an hour before using

Method

1. Combine the marinade ingredients—chopped onion, Worcestershire sauce, minced garlic, and soy sauce then pour water into the mixture. Stir well then set aside.

2. Next, combine the rub ingredients—brown sugar, sweet paprika, salt, chili powder, mustard, black pepper, and ginger in a bowl then mix well. Set aside.

3. After that, combine apple juice with water, Worcestershire sauce, salt, and granulated sugar. Stir vigorously until the sugar and salt are completely dissolved.

4. Fill an injector with the mixture then inject the pork butt in several places.

5. Rub the pork butt with the marinade mixture then sprinkle the rub mixture all over the pork butt.

6. Light a fire in a ceramic smoker with charcoal and soaked Cherry wood chips then preheat to 225°F (107°C).

7. Set a rack in the ceramic smoker then place a ceramic smoker and a grate in it.

8. Once the ceramic smoker has reached the desired temperature, place the seasoned pork butt on the grate and smoke the pork butt for 6 hours.

9. Meanwhile, combine apple juice with water and cider vinegar then spray over the pork butt once every hour.

10. Once the internal temperature of the pork butt has reached 195°F (91°C), remove the smoked pork butt from the ceramic smoker.

11. Place the smoked pork butt on a serving dish then cut using a fork.

12. Serve and enjoy.

Smoked Pork Ribs with Apple Aroma

(total cook time 4 hours 50 minutes)

Ingredients for 10 servings

- Pork Ribs (5-lbs., 2.3-kgs)

The Rub

- Salt – 2 teaspoons
- Brown sugar – ½ cup
- Pepper – 2 teaspoons
- Chili powder – 3 tablespoons
- Cayenne powder – 2 teaspoons
- Garlic powder – 1 tablespoon

- Onion powder – 2 tablespoons
- Mustard – 1 teaspoon
- Paprika – 2 teaspoons

THE GLAZE

- Apple juice – 1 cup

THE WATER PAN

- Apple juice – 3 cups

THE FIRE

- Preheat a smoker an hour prior to smoking.
- Use charcoal Apple woods for smoking.
- Soak the Apple wood chips for about an hour before using

METHOD

1. Combine salt with brown sugar, pepper, chili powder, cayenne powder, garlic powder, onion powder, mustard, and paprika then mix well.
2. Rub the pork ribs with the spice mixture then place in a zipper-lock plastic bag.
3. Let the pork ribs rest overnight and store in the fridge to keep it fresh.
4. On the next day, remove the seasoned pork ribs from the fridge then thaw at room temperature.
5. Light a fire in a ceramic smoker with charcoal and soaked Apple wood chips.
6. Set a rack in the ceramic smoker and place a ceramic plate in the smoker.
7. Pour Apple juice into a disposable aluminum pan then place in on the ceramic plate.
8. Set the grate on top then preheat the ceramic smoker to 250°F (121°C).
9. Once the smoker has reached the desired temperature, take the seasoned pork ribs from the zipper-lock plastic bag then place directly on the grate.
10. Smoke the pork ribs for 4 hours or until the internal temperature has reached 165°F (74°C). Use the vent to control the heat.

11. After 4 hours, take the smoked pork ribs out of the ceramic smoker then place on a sheet of aluminum foil.

12. Spray Apple juice all over the smoked pork ribs then tightly wrap it with aluminum foil.

13. Return the wrapped smoked pork ribs to the ceramic smoker then smoke for 30 minutes.

14. Once it is done, remove from the ceramic smoker and let it rest for about 20 minutes.

15. Unwrap the smoked pork ribs then transfer to a serving dish.

16. Serve and enjoy.

Hickory Sweet Honey Smoked Pulled Pork

(Total cook time 4 hours 10 minutes)

Ingredients for 10 servings

- Pork shoulder (3-lbs., 1.4-kgs)

The Rub

- Brown sugar – 2 tablespoons
- Garlic powder – 2 tablespoons
- Black pepper – 2 tablespoons
- Thyme – 2 tablespoons
- Oregano – 3 tablespoons
- Salt – 1 ½ teaspoons
- Chili powder – 2 tablespoons
- Fennel seeds – ¼ teaspoon
- Paprika – ¾ teaspoon

The Glaze

- Butter – ¼ cup
- Honey – ½ cup

The Fire

- Preheat a smoker an hour prior to smoking.
- Use charcoal Hickory woods for smoking.
- Soak the Hickory wood chips for about an hour before using

Method

1. Place the rub ingredients—brown sugar, garlic powder, black pepper, thyme, oregano, salt, chili powder, fennel seeds, and paprika in a bowl. Stir until combined.
2. Cut and trim the excess fats from the pork shoulder then rub with the spice mixture. Let it rest overnight and store in the fridge to keep it fresh.
3. In the morning, remove the seasoned pork shoulder from the fridge and thaw at room temperature.
4. Place charcoal and soaked Hickory wood chips in a ceramic smoker then light a fire in it.

5. Preheat the ceramic smoker to 250°F (121°C) and set a rack with the ceramic plate in it.

6. Place a water pan on the ceramic plate then set the grate on it.

7. Once the smoker has reached the desired temperature, place the seasoned pork shoulder on the grate and smoke for 2 hours.

8. Meanwhile, melt butter and combine with honey. Stir until incorporated.

9. After 2 hours of smoking, remove the pork shoulder from the ceramic smoker then place on a sheet of aluminum foil.

10. Baste the pork shoulder with the butter and honey mixture then tightly wrap with aluminum foil.

11. Return the pork shoulder to the ceramic smoker then smoke for another 2 hours or until the internal temperature has reached 165°F (74°C). Use the vent to control the temperature.

12. Once the smoked pork is done, remove from the ceramic smoker.

13. Let the smoked pork rest for a bout 15 minutes then unwrap it.

14. Using a fork shred the smoked pork and place on a serving dish.

15. Serve and enjoy.

Smoked Pork Belly with Black Sauce

(Total cook time 5 hours 10 minutes)

Ingredients for 10 servings

- Pork belly (2.5-lbs., 1.1-kgs)

The Rub

- Black pepper – 2 teaspoons
- Fennel seeds – ½ teaspoon
- Cilantro – 1 teaspoon
- All spice – ½ teaspoon
- Cumin – 1 teaspoon
- Brown sugar – 3 tablespoons

THE SAUCE

- Water – 1 ½ cups
- Chopped onion – ½ cup
- Chili powder – ½ teaspoon
- Ginger – ½ teaspoon
- Soy sauce – 1 cup
- Dark rice vinegar – 1 cup
- Olive oil – 1 tablespoon
- Lemon grass – 2
- Honey – ¼ cup
- Minced garlic – 2 teaspoons

THE FIRE

- Preheat a smoker an hour prior to smoking.
- Use charcoal Lilac woods for smoking.
- Soak the Lilac wood chips for about an hour before using

METHOD

1. Mix the spices in a bowl—black pepper, fennel seeds, cilantro, all spice, cumin, brown sugar in a bowl then mix until combined.
2. Cut the pork belly into big cubes then roll in the spice mixture. Let the pork belly rest for 2 hours.
3. Place charcoal and soaked Lilac wood chips in the ceramic smoker then prepare for indirect heat.
4. Light a fire in the ceramic smoker then wait until the ceramic smoker has reached 250°F (121°C).
5. Arrange the seasoned pork belly on the grate and smoke for 3 hours.
6. In the meantime, make the sauce.
7. Preheat a saucepan and pour olive oil into it.

8. Once the oil is hot, stir in minced garlic then sauté until aromatic.

9. Add the remaining sauce ingredients then stir well. Bring to a simmer then remove from heat.

10. Transfer the sauce to a disposable aluminum pan then let it cool.

11. After 3 hours of smoking, remove the pork belly from the ceramic smoker and transfer to the aluminum pan with the sauce.

12. Place the aluminum pan with pork belly in the ceramic smoker then smoke the pork belly for 2 hours.

13. Once it is done, remove the smoked pork belly to a serving dish then drizzle the remaining sauce over the smoked pork belly.

14. Serve and enjoy.

Peach Glazed Smoked Pork Loin

(Total cook time 5 hours 10 minutes)

Ingredients for 10 servings

- Pork loin (3.5-lbs., 1.6-kgs)

The Rub

- Salt – 1 teaspoon
- Brown sugar – 3 tablespoons
- Garlic powder – 2 ½ teaspoons
- Onion powder – 2 teaspoons
- Grated lemon zest – 1 teaspoon

THE GLAZE

- Peach preserves – 1 cup
- Mustard – ¼ cup
- Onion powder – ½ tablespoon
- Garlic powder – ½ tablespoon

THE FIRE

- Preheat a smoker an hour prior to smoking.
- Use charcoal Hickory woods for smoking.
- Soak the Hickory wood chips for about an hour before using

METHOD

1. Rub the pork loin with salt, brown sugar, garlic powder, onion powder, and grated lemon zest then let it rest for about an hour.
2. Combine peach preserves with mustard, onion powder, and garlic powder then stir until incorporated. Set aside.
3. Light a fire in a ceramic smoker with charcoal and soaked Hickory wood chips. Prepare for indirect heat.
4. Wait until the ceramic smoker has reached 300°F (148°C) and place the seasoned pork loin on the grate.
5. Smoke the pork loin for 5 hours and baste with the peach glaze once every hour.
6. Once the internal temperature of the smoked pork loin has reached 145°F (63°C), remove the smoked pork loin from the ceramic smoker.
7. Transfer to a serving dish then cut into slices.
8. Drizzle the remaining Peach glaze on top.
9. Serve and enjoy.

LAMB

Smoked Lemon Lamb Leg Marjoram

(Total cook time 3 hours 40 minutes)

Ingredients for 10 servings

- Lamb leg (4.5-lbs., 2-kgs)

The Rub

- Olive oil – 3 tablespoons
- Chopped rosemary – ¼ cup
- Thyme – ¼ cup
- Chopped parsley – ¼ cup
- Marjoram – ¼ cup

- Cumin – 2 teaspoons
- Minced garlic – 3 tablespoons
- Grated lemon zest – 2 teaspoons
- Balsamic vinegar – 2 teaspoons

THE FIRE

- Preheat a smoker an hour prior to smoking.
- Use charcoal Apple woods for smoking.
- Soak the Apple wood chips for about an hour before using

METHOD

1. Combine the rub ingredients—olive oil, chopped rosemary, thyme, chopped parsley, marjoram, cumin, minced garlic, grated lemon zest, and balsamic vinegar in a bowl. Mix well.
2. Score the lamb leg at several places then rub with the spice mixture. Let it rest for an hour.
3. Prepare a ceramic smoker for indirect heat with charcoal and soaked Apple wood chips.
4. Light a fire in the ceramic smoker and preheat it to 300°F (148°C). Use the vent to control the temperature.
5. Once the ceramic temperature has reached the desired temperature, place the seasoned lamb leg on the grate.
6. Smoke the lamb leg for approximately 3 hours and a half or until the internal temperature has reached 145°F (63°C) for medium doneness. If you want it to be well done, continue smoking until the internal temperature has reached 1658F (74°C).
7. Once the smoked lamb leg is done, remove from the ceramic smoker then let it rest for 10 minutes.
8. Cut into slices and transfer to a serving dish.
9. Serve and enjoy.

SMOKED LAMB RIBS WITH APRICOT GLAZE

(TOTAL COOK TIME 4 HOURS 10 MINUTES)

INGREDIENTS FOR 10 SERVINGS

- Lamb ribs (4-lbs., 1.8-kgs)

THE RUB

- Butter – 3 tablespoons
- Salt – 2 teaspoons
- Pepper – 2 teaspoons
- Oregano – 1 teaspoon
- Rosemary – 1 teaspoon
- Thyme – 1 teaspoon
- Cayenne pepper – 1 teaspoon
- Chili powder – 1 teaspoon

THE GLAZE

- Barbecue sauce – 1 cup
- Apricot preserves – ¼ cup
- Apple juice – ¼ cup

THE FIRE

- Preheat a smoker an hour prior to smoking.
- Use charcoal Cherry woods for smoking.
- Soak the Cherry wood chips for about an hour before using

METHOD

1. Make some scores at the lamb ribs then baste butter all over the lamb ribs.
2. Sprinkle salt, pepper, oregano, rosemary, thyme, cayenne pepper, and chili powder over the lamb ribs then let it sit for about an hour.
3. Prepare a ceramic smoker for indirect heat and preheat to 250°F (121°C). Use charcoal and soaked Cherry wood chips to create smokes.

4. Set the rack in the ceramic smoker then insert a ceramic plate and a grate in it.

5. Once the ceramic smoker has reached the desired temperature, place the seasoned lamb ribs on the grate. Smoke the lamb ribs for 3 hours.

6. In the meantime, combine barbecue sauce with apricot preserves and apple juice then stir until incorporated. Set aside.

7. After 3 hours, remove the lamb ribs from the ceramic smoker then place on a sheet of aluminum foil.

8. Baste the lamb ribs with the apricot glaze then wrap with aluminum foil.

9. Return the wrapped lamb ribs to the ceramic smoker and smoke for 2 hours. Maintain the temperature at 250°F (121°C).

10. Smoke the lamb ribs until the internal temperature has reached 165°F (74°C).

11. Remove the smoked lamb ribs from the ceramic smoker then let it sit for about 15 minutes.

12. Unwrap the smoked lamb ribs then transfer to a serving dish.

13. Baste the remaining apricot glaze over the smoked lamb ribs then serve.

14. Enjoy!

MILKY SMOKED LAMB CHOPS WITH WHITE SAUCE

(TOTAL COOK TIME 20 MINUTES)

INGREDIENTS FOR 10 SERVINGS

- Lamb chops (3-lbs., 1.4-kgs)

THE MARINADE

- Plain yogurt – 1 ½ cups
- Grated lemon zest – 1 teaspoon
- Lemon juice – ¼ cup
- Minced garlic – 3 tablespoons

- Cinnamon – ¾ tablespoon
- Oregano – 1 tablespoon
- Chopped rosemary – ¼ cup
- Salt – 2 teaspoons
- Pepper – ¾ tablespoon

THE SAUCE

- White wine – 1 cup
- Sliced shallots – ¼ cup
- Whipped cream – 2 cups
- Dijon mustard – ¼ cup
- Chopped rosemary – 1 tablespoon

THE FIRE

- Preheat a smoker an hour prior to smoking.
- Use charcoal Cherry woods for smoking.
- Soak the Cherry wood chips for about an hour before using

METHOD

1. Cut the lamb chops into 2-inches cubes then place in a zipper-lock plastic bag.
2. Place minced garlic, cinnamon, oregano, chopped rosemary, salt, and pepper in a bowl.
3. Pour yogurt and lemon juice over the spice then stir until combined.
4. Pour the spice mixture into the zipper-lock plastic bag then shake until the lamb chops are completely coated with the spice mixture.
5. Marinate the lamb chops overnight and store in the fridge to keep them fresh.
6. On the next day, remove the lamb chops from the fridge then thaw at room temperature.
7. Light a fire in ceramic smoker with charcoal and cherry wood chips then preheat it to 400°F (204°C). Use the vent to control the temperature.

8. Once the ceramic smoker is ready, place the seasoned lamb chops on the grate then smoke for 10 minutes.

9. After 10 minutes, flip the lamb chops and smoke for 10 minutes more.

10. Meanwhile, pour white wine into a saucepan and add sliced shallots to the saucepan. Bring to boil.

11. Pour whipped cream into the saucepan then cook for 10 minutes until the mixture is thickened.

12. Add Dijon mustard and chopped rosemary to the saucepan then bring to a simmer.

13. Remove the sauce from heat then set aside.

14. Once the lamb chops are done, remove the smoked lamb chops from the ceramic smoker then place on a serving dish.

15. Drizzle white sauce over the smoked lamb chops then serve.

16. Enjoy!

Cheesy Smoked Lamb Roast with Orange Marinade

(TOTAL COOK TIME 1 HOUR 30 MINUTES)

Ingredients for 10 servings

- Boneless lamb leg (2-lbs., 0.9-kgs)

The Marinade

- Orange juice – 1 cup
- Red wine – 2 cups
- Minced garlic – ¼ cup
- Thyme – 2 tablespoons
- Black pepper – 2 teaspoons

THE FILLING

- Salt – 1 teaspoon
- Pepper – 1 teaspoon
- Crumbled blue cheese – ¼ cup

THE FIRE

- Preheat a smoker an hour prior to smoking.
- Use charcoal Oak wood chips for smoking.
- Soak the Oak wood chips for about an hour before using

METHOD

1. Combine orange juice with red wine in a bowl then add minced garlic, thyme, and black pepper. Stir until incorporated.
2. Place the boneless lamb leg in a zipper-lock plastic bag then pour the spice mixture into the plastic bag. Shake until the lamb leg is coated with the spice mixture.
3. Marinate the lamb leg overnight and store in the refrigerator to keep it fresh.
4. In the morning, remove the lamb leg from the refrigerator then thaw at room temperature.
5. Cut the boneless lamb leg into a large thin slice then place on a flat surface.
6. Sprinkle salt, pepper, and crumbled blue cheese then roll the lamb.
7. Place the rolled lamb in a disposable aluminum pan then set aside.
8. Place charcoal and soaked Oak wood chips in the ceramic smoker.
9. Light a fire in the ceramic smoker and preheat to 325°F (163°C).
10. Once the ceramic smoker is ready, place the aluminum pan with rolled lamb leg on the grated then smoke for an hour and a half.
11. When the internal temperature of the smoked lamb has reached 145°F (63°C), remove it from the ceramic smoker.
12. Cut the smoked lamb into slices then serve. Enjoy!

Spiced Smoked Lamb Tender

(Total cook time 4 hours 10 minutes)

Ingredients for 10 servings

- Boneless lamb leg (2.5-lbs., 1.1-kgs)

The Brine

- Water – 4 cups
- Lemon juice – 5 tablespoons
- Fresh oranges – 2
- Peppercorns – ½ cup
- Minced garlic – 2 tablespoons
- Thyme – 1 tablespoon

- Rosemary – 1 tablespoon
- Salt – ½ cup
- Sugar – ½ cup

THE RUB

- Cumin – 1 teaspoon
- Cardamom – 1 teaspoon
- Turmeric – 1 teaspoon
- Salt – 1 teaspoon
- Pepper – 1 teaspoon
- Garlic powder – 1 teaspoon
- Ginger – ½ teaspoon
- Nutmeg – ½ teaspoon
- Allspice – ½ teaspoon
- Mustard – ½ teaspoon
- Coriander – ½ teaspoon
- Red chili flakes – 2 tablespoons
- Cayenne pepper – ¼ teaspoon
- White vinegar – ¼ cup

THE FIRE

- Preheat a smoker an hour prior to smoking.
- Use charcoal and Oak wood chips for smoking.
- Soak the Oak wood chips for about an hour before using

METHOD

1. Pour water and lemon juice in a container then add peppercorns, minced garlic, thyme, rosemary, salt, and sugar to the container. Stir until the spices are completely dissolved.

2. Cut the fresh oranges into slices then add to the container. Stir until just combined.

3. Add the boneless lamb leg to the container and submerge it in the brine overnight. Store in the refrigerator to keep it fresh.

4. On the next day, remove the lamb leg from the refrigerator then wash and rinse it. Pat it dry.

5. Combine the rub ingredients—cumin, cardamom, turmeric, salt, pepper, garlic powder, ginger, nutmeg, allspice, mustard, coriander, red chili flakes, cayenne pepper, and white vinegar in a bowl then mix well.

6. Rub the boneless lamb leg with the spice mixture then let it rest.

7. Prepare a ceramic smoker for indirect heat with charcoal and soaked Oak wood chips then preheat it to 325°F (163°C). Use the vent to control the heat.

8. Set the rack in the ceramic smoker completed with the ceramic plate and grate.

9. Once the ceramic smoker reaches the desired temperature, place the seasoned boneless lamb leg on the grate.

10. Smoke the boneless lamb leg for 4 hours and once it is done, remove from the ceramic smoker. The internal temperature of the smoked boneless lamb leg will be 163°F (74°C0.

11. Let the smoked lamb led for about 15 minutes then cut into slices.

12. Serve and enjoy.

FISH
Lemon Rosemary Smoked Sardines

(Total cook time 2 Hours 10 minutes)

Ingredients for 10 servings

- Fresh whole sardines (3-lbs., 1.4-kgs)

The Rub

- Olive oil – ¼ cup
- Salt – 2 tablespoons
- Pepper – 2 teaspoons
- Minced garlic – 2 tablespoons
- Chopped parsley – 3 tablespoons

THE FILLING

- Fresh rosemary – ½ cup

THE GLAZE

- Lemon juice – ¼ cup

THE FIRE

- Preheat a smoker an hour prior to smoking.
- Use charcoal Peach woods for smoking.
- Soak the Peach wood chips before using

METHOD

1. Combine salt, pepper, minced garlic, and chopped parsley in a bowl.
2. Pour olive oil over the spices then mix well.
3. Rub the sardines with the spice mixture then fill each sardine cavity with fresh rosemary.
4. Place charcoal and soaked Peach wood chips in a ceramic smoker and light a fire in it.
5. Set the rack in the position then place a ceramic plate and a grate on it.
6. Close the ceramic smoker and preheat the ceramic smoker to 250°F (121°C).
7. Once the ceramic smoker reaches the desired temperature, arrange the seasoned sardines on the grate.
8. Close the ceramic smoker and smoke the sardines for 2 hours or until the internal temperature has reached 145°F (63°C).
9. When the smoked sardines are done, remove from the ceramic smoker and quickly brush or spray lemon juice over the smoked sardines.
10. Serve and enjoy.

Buttery Smoked Salmon Black Pepper

(total cook time 2 hours 10 minutes)

Ingredients for 10 servings

- Salmon fillet (2.5-lbs., 1.1-kgs)

The Rub

- Butter – ½ cup
- Tamari – 1 cup
- Worcestershire sauce – 1 cup
- Sesame oil – ¼ cup
- Garlic powder – 2 tablespoons
- Italian seasoning – 2 tablespoons

- Ginger – 2 teaspoons
- Basil – 2 teaspoons
- Ground black pepper – 2 tablespoons

THE FIRE

- Preheat a smoker an hour prior to smoking.
- Use charcoal and Pear wood chips for smoking.
- Soak the Pear wood chips before using

METHOD

1. Melt butter over medium heat then add tamari, Worcestershire sauce, sesame oil, garlic powder, Italian seasoning, ginger, and basil. Stir well.
2. Baste the salmon fillet with spice mixture then arrange in a disposable aluminum pan.
3. Sprinkle ground black pepper over the salmon fillet then drizzle the remaining spice mixture on top. Set aside.
4. Place charcoal and soaked Pear wood chips in a ceramic smoker and light a fire in it.
5. Set the rack in the position then place a ceramic plate and a grate on it.
6. Close the ceramic smoker and preheat the ceramic smoker to 225°F (107°C).
7. Once the ceramic smoker reaches the desired temperature, place the aluminum pan with salmon fillet on the grate.
8. Close the ceramic smoker and smoke the salmon fillet for an hour.
9. After an hour, take the aluminum pan out of the smoker.
10. Take the salmon fillet out of the aluminum pan and arrange directly on the grate.
11. Smoke the salmon fillet again for an hour or until the internal temperature has reached 145°F (63°C).
12. Once it is done, remove from the smoker then arrange the smoked salmon fillet on a serving dish.
13. Serve and enjoy.

Lemon Smoked Red Snapper with Fresh Dill and Rosemary

(Total cook time 2 hours 10 minutes)

Ingredients for 10 servings

- Fresh whole red snapper (3-lbs., 1.4-kgs)

The Spice

- Lemon juice – 3 tablespoons
- Black pepper – 2 teaspoons
- Salt – 1 ½ teaspoons
- Olive oil – 3 tablespoons

THE FILLING

- Sliced lemon – ½ cup
- Fresh rosemary – ¼ cup
- Fresh dill – ¼ cup
- Sliced onion – ½ cup

THE FIRE

- Preheat a smoker an hour prior to smoking.
- Use charcoal and Alder woods for smoking.
- Soak the Alder wood chips before using

METHOD

1. Score the fresh snapper at several places then rub with lemon juice. Let it sit for a few minutes.
2. Prepare a ceramic smoker for indirect heat with charcoal and soaked Alder wood chips.
3. Light a fire in the ceramic smoker then set a rack and place a ceramic plate in it.
4. Preheat the ceramic smoker to 200°F (93°C) and wait until it reaches the desired temperature.
5. Spread sliced onion in the bottom of a disposable aluminum pan then place the snapper on it.
6. Fill the snapper cavity with fresh rosemary and dill then insert sliced lemon at the snapper.
7. Sprinkle salt and pepper over the snapper then drizzle olive oil on top.
8. Place the disposable aluminum pan with snapper on the ceramic plate then smoke the snapper for 2 hours.
9. Once it is done, remove the smoked snapper from the ceramic smoker and transfer to a serving dish.
10. Serve and enjoy.

CITRUS SMOKED KIPPER WITH SOY SAUCE

(TOTAL COOK TIME 20 MINUTES)

INGREDIENTS FOR 10 SERVINGS

- Kipper fillet (2 lbs., 0.9-kgs)

THE SPICE

- Citrus – ½ cup
- Salt – 1 ½ teaspoons
- Pepper – 2 teaspoons

THE SAUCE

- Butter – 2 tablespoon

- Lemon juice – 2 tablespoons
- Soy sauce – ½ cup

THE FIRE

- Preheat a smoker an hour prior to smoking.
- Use charcoal and Alder woods for smoking.
- Soak the Alder wood chips before using

METHOD

1. Prepare a ceramic smoker for indirect heat with charcoal and smoked Alder wood chips.
2. Light a fire in the ceramic smoker and set the rack in it.
3. Place a ceramic plate in the ceramic smoker and wait until the ceramic smoker has reached 250°F (121°C).
4. Cut the kipper fillet into thin slices then place in a disposable aluminum pan.
5. Drizzle citrus over the kipper fillet then sprinkle salt and pepper on top.
6. Once the ceramic smoker is ready, place the aluminum pan with kipper fillet in the ceramic smoker and smoke for 20 minutes.
7. In the meantime, melt butter then combine with lemon juice and soy sauce. Stir well.
8. Once the smoked kipper is done, remove from the ceramic smoker then quickly baste the sauce over the smoked kipper.
9. Serve and enjoy.

SEAFOOD
SMOKED SHRIMP SKEWER CURRY

(TOTAL COOK TIME 10 MINUTES)

INGREDIENTS FOR 10 SERVINGS

- Fresh shrimps (2.5-lbs., 1.1-kgs)

THE MARINADE

- Orange juice – ½ cup
- Honey – 6 tablespoons
- Soy sauce – ¼ cup
- Sesame oil – 1 ½ tablespoons

- Chili sauce – 1 ½ tablespoons
- Salt – 1 tablespoon
- Curry powder – ½ tablespoon
- Ginger – ½ tablespoon
- Minced garlic – ½ tablespoon

THE FIRE

- Preheat a smoker an hour prior to smoking.
- Use charcoal and Alder wood chips for smoking.
- Soak the Alder wood chips before using

METHOD

1. Combine the marinade ingredients—orange juice, honey, soy sauce, sesame oil, chili sauce, salt, curry powder, ginger, and minced garlic in a container then stir until incorporated.
2. Peel the fresh shrimps then remove the head.
3. Add the shrimps to the spice mixture then marinate for 30 minutes.
4. In the meantime, prepare a ceramic smoker for indirect heat with charcoal and soaked Alder woods.
5. Set the rack completed with the ceramic plate and the grate then preheat the ceramic smoker to 250°F (121°C).
6. Prick the seasoned shrimps with stainless steel skewers and once the ceramic smoker has reached the desired temperature, place the shrimps on the grate.
7. Smoke the seasoned shrimps for 5 minutes then flip the shrimps.
8. Smoke the shrimps for 5 minutes more then remove from the ceramic smoker. The internal temperature of the smoked shrimps will be 145°F (63°C) at this time.
9. Arrange the smoked shrimps on a serving dish then serve.
10. Enjoy!

SMOKED SCALLOP CHILI

(TOTAL COOK TIME 10 MINUTES)

INGREDIENTS FOR 10 SERVINGS

- Scallops (2-lbs., 0.9-kgs)

THE SPICE

- Lemon juice – ¼ cup
- Grated lemon zest – 1 teaspoon
- Salt – ½ teaspoon
- Pepper – ½ teaspoon

THE GLAZE

- Olive oil – 2 tablespoons

THE FIRE

- Preheat a smoker an hour prior to smoking.
- Use charcoal Alder wood chips for smoking.
- Soak the Alder wood chips before using

METHOD

1. Drizzle lemon juice over the scallops then rub them with salt, pepper, and grated lemon zest.
2. Marinate the scallops for an hour and store in the fridge to keep them fresh.
3. Preheat a ceramic smoker to 300°F (148°C) and set the rack with ceramic plate and the grate.
4. Once the ceramic smoker is read, arrange the marinated scallops on the grate.
5. Smoke the scallops for 4 minutes then flip them and smoke again for another 4 minutes.
6. Once it is done, remove the smoked scallops from the ceramic smoked then serve and enjoy.

Gingery Smoked Oyster Alder

(Total cook time 1 hour 15 minutes)

Ingredients for 10 servings

- Oyster (1.5 lbs., 0.7-kgs)

The Rub

- Lemon juice – 2 tablespoons
- Ginger – 1 ½ teaspoons
- Salt – ½ teaspoon
- Pepper – ½ teaspoon

THE FIRE

- Preheat a smoker an hour prior to smoking.
- Use charcoal and Alder wood chips for smoking.
- Soak the Alder wood chips before using

METHOD

1. Place charcoal and soaked Alder wood chips in a ceramic smoker then light a fire in it.
2. Preheat the ceramic smoker to 225°F (107°C) and set the rack in it.
3. Rub the oysters with lemon juice, ginger, salt, and pepper then wrap with aluminum foil.
4. Place the wrapped oysters in the ceramic smoker and smoke for an hour.
5. Once it is done, remove from the ceramic smoker then let them sit wrapped for about 10 minutes.
6. Unwrap the smoked oysters then transfer to a serving dish.
7. Serve and enjoy.

Lemon Smoked Mussel Rosemary

(TOTAL COOK TIME 1 HOUR 5 MINUTES)

Ingredients for 10 servings

- Mussels (3-lbs., 1.4-kgs)

The Spice

- Butter – ½ cup
- Chopped onion – ½ cup
- Minced garlic – 2 teaspoons
- Thyme – 1 teaspoon
- Lemon juice – 2 cups
- Water – ½ cup
- Grated lemon zest – 2 tablespoons

THE TOPPING

- Chopped rosemary – 3 tablespoons

THE FIRE

- Preheat a smoker an hour prior to smoking.
- Use charcoal and Mesquite wood chips for smoking.
- Soak the Mesquite wood chips before using.

METHOD

1. Preheat a saucepan over medium heat then melt butter in it.
2. Stir in chopped onion and minced garlic to the saucepan then sauté until wilted and aromatic.
3. Remove from heat then add thyme, lemon juice, water, and grated lemon zest to the saucepan then stir well.
4. Place the mussels in a disposable aluminum pan then drizzle the butter mixture over the mussels. Stir until the mussels are completely coated with butter.
5. Prepare a ceramic smoker for indirect heat with charcoal and Mesquite wood chips.
6. Preheat the ceramic smoker to 225°F (107°C) and wait until it reaches the desired temperature.
7. Sprinkle chopped rosemary over the mussels then place in the ceramic smoker.
8. Smoke the mussels for an hour and once the mussels are tender, remove from the ceramic smoker.
9. Transfer to a serving dish then enjoy.

VEGETABLES

SMOKED EGGPLANT PAPRIKA WITH OREGANO

(TOTAL COOK TIME 1 HOUR 5 MINUTES)

INGREDIENTS FOR 10 SERVINGS

- Eggplants (1.5-lbs., 0.7-kgs)

THE SPICE

- Minced garlic – 5 tablespoons
- Oregano – 1 tablespoon
- Basil – 1 tablespoon

- Chopped thyme – 1 tablespoon
- Smoked paprika – 1 tablespoon
- Red chili flakes – 1 tablespoon
- Salt – 1 teaspoon
- Black pepper – 1 ½ teaspoons

THE FIRE

- Preheat a smoker an hour prior to smoking.
- Use charcoal and Pear wood chips for smoking.
- Soak the Pear wood chips before using.

METHOD

1. Combine minced garlic with oregano, basil, chopped thyme, smoked paprika, red chili flakes, salt, and black pepper in a bowl. Mix well.
2. Cut the eggplants into halves lengthwise then rub with the spice mixture.
3. Prepare a ceramic smoker for indirect heat with charcoal and soaked Pear wood chips.
4. Set the rack in the ceramic smoker completed with the ceramic plate and the grate then wait until the ceramic smoker has reached 250°F (121°C).
5. Arrange the halved eggplants in a disposable aluminum pan the place in the ceramic smoker.
6. Smoke the eggplants for an hour or until the smoked eggplants are tender. The smoking time will vary according to the size of the eggplants.
7. Once the smoked eggplants are done, remove from the ceramic smoker and transfer to a serving dish.
8. Serve and enjoy.

SMOKED RED TOMATO GARLIC

(TOTAL COOK TIME 15 MINUTES)

INGREDIENTS FOR 10 SERVINGS

- Red Tomato (2-lbs., 0.9-kgs)

The Spice

- Minced garlic – 1 tablespoon
- Honey – 2 tablespoons
- Balsamic vinegar – 2 tablespoons
- Salt – ½ teaspoon
- Pepper – ½ teaspoon
- Chopped parsley – 1 tablespoon

The Fire

- Preheat a smoker an hour prior to smoking.
- Use charcoal and Pear wood chips for smoking.
- Soak the Pear wood chips before using.

Method

1. Combine minced garlic with balsamic vinegar, salt and pepper then mix well.
2. Cut the tomatoes into halves then arrange in a disposable aluminum pan with the cut side up.
3. Drizzle honey on over the tomatoes then sprinkle the spice mixture and chopped parsley on top. Set aside.
4. Place charcoal and soaked Pear wood in a ceramic smoker then light a fire in it.
5. Set the rack in the ceramic smoker then preheat the ceramic smoker to 250°F (121°C).
6. Once the ceramic smoker is ready, place the disposable aluminum pan in the ceramic smoker and smoke the tomatoes for 15-20 minutes.
7. Remove the smoked tomatoes from the ceramic smoker and transfer to a serving dish.
8. Serve and enjoy.

Bacon Stuffed Smoked Cabbage

(TOTAL COOK TIME 1 HOUR 5 MINUTES)

Ingredients for 10 servings

- Cabbage (1.5-lbs., 0.7-kgs)

The Filling

- Butter – ¼ cup
- Chili powder – 2 teaspoons
- Oregano – 1 teas
- Garlic powder – 2 teaspoons
- Cumin – 1 teaspoon
- Diced bacon – ¼ cup
- Chicken broth – 3 tablespoons

THE FIRE

- Preheat a smoker an hour prior to smoking.
- Use charcoal and Pear wood chips for smoking.
- Soak the Pear wood chips before using.

METHOD

1. Place the butter in a bowl then stir until softened.
2. Add chili powder, oregano, cumin, and garlic powder then mix well.
3. Add diced bacon to the butter then stir until combined.
4. Core the cabbage and make a hole at the cabbage.
5. Fill the hole with the bacon mixture then wrap the aluminum foil. Let the topside open.
6. Pour chicken broth over the cabbage then set aside.
7. Prepare a ceramic smoker for indirect heat and preheat it to 250°F (121°C). Use charcoal and soaked wood chips to create smokes.
8. Once the smoker has reached the desired temperature, place the wrapped cabbage on the grate then smoke the cabbage for an hour. The smoking time will vary depending on the size of the cabbage.
9. Remove the smoked cabbage from the smoker and unwrap it. The cabbage should be tender at this time.
10. Cut the smoked cabbage into wedges then serve.
11. Enjoy warm.

Juicy Smoked Onion with Whiskey Glaze

(TOTAL COOK TIME 2 HOURS 5 MINUTES)

Ingredients for 10 servings

- Onion 8 (2-lbs., 0.9-kgs)

The Rub

- Olive oil – ¼ cup

The Glaze

- Beef broth – 1 ¼ cups
- Whiskey – 6 tablespoons

- Steak seasoning – ¾ tablespoon
- Thyme – ¾ teaspoon

THE FIRE

- Preheat a smoker an hour prior to smoking.
- Use charcoal and Oak wood chips for smoking.
- Soak the Oak wood chips before using.

METHOD

1. Prepare a ceramic smoker for indirect heat with charcoal and soaked wood chips.
2. Set the rack in the ceramic smoker completed with the ceramic plate and grate then wait until the ceramic smoker has reached 250°F (121°C).
3. In the meantime, combine beef broth with whiskey then add steak seasoning and thyme to the broth mixture. Stir until incorporated.
4. Cut the onions into halves then place in a disposable aluminum pan.
5. Rub the halved onions with olive oil then place the aluminum pan in the ceramic smoker.
6. Smoke the onions for 2 hours and baste with the glaze mixture once every 30 minutes.
7. Once it is done, remove the smoked onions from the ceramic smoker then transfer to a serving dish.
8. Serve and enjoy.

CHICKEN

Smoked Chicken Breast with Strawberry Glaze

(total cook time 3 Hours 45 minutes)

Ingredients for 10 servings

- Boneless chicken breast (5-lbs., 2.3-kgs)

The Rub

- Chopped rosemary – 3 teaspoons
- Salt – 2 tablespoons
- Ground black pepper – 2 ½ teaspoons
- Chopped thyme – 2 ½ teaspoons

The Glaze

- Balsamic vinegar – ¼ cup
- Strawberry preserves – ½ cup

THE FIRE

- Preheat a smoker an hour prior to smoking.
- Use charcoal Cherry woods for smoking.
- Soak the Cherry wood chips before using

METHOD

1. Score the boneless chicken breast in several places then place on a flat surface.
2. Sprinkle salt over the boneless chicken breast then rub with chopped rosemary, black pepper, and thyme.
3. Wrap the seasoned chicken breast with plastic wrap then let it sit for 2 hours. Store in the fridge to keep it fresh.
4. Meanwhile, place strawberry preserves in a saucepan then pour balsamic vinegar over the strawberry preserves. Stir well and bring to a simmer.
5. After 2 hours, remove the seasoned chicken breast then thaw at room temperature. Unwrap the chicken breast.
6. In the meantime, place charcoal and soaked Cherry wood chips in a ceramic smoker then light a fire in it.
7. Set the rack in the smoker then insert ceramic plate and grate in it. Close the smoker.
8. Preheat the ceramic smoker to 300°F (148°C) and wait until it reaches the desired temperature.
9. Once the ceramic smoker is ready, place the seasoned chicken breast on the grate with the skin side down.
10. Smoke the chicken breast for an hour and a half then open the ceramic smoker.
11. Baste the chicken breast with the strawberry mixture then smoke again for about 2 hours and 15 minutes.
12. Once the internal temperature of the smoked chicken breast has reached 165°F (74°C), remove the smoked chicken breast from the smoker.
13. Serve and enjoy.

Spicy Smoked Chicken Wings

(Total cook time 3 Hours 45 minutes)

Ingredients for 10 servings

- Chicken Wings (2.5-lbs., 1.1-kgs)

The Rub

- Garlic powder – 3 tablespoons
- Smoked paprika – 3 tablespoons
- Kosher salt – 3 tablespoons
- Cayenne pepper – 3 tablespoons
- Onion powder – 1 ½ tablespoons
- Pepper – 1 teaspoon

The Glaze

- Honey – ¾ cup
- Barbecue sauce – ¼ cup
- Apple juice – 2 tablespoons

THE FIRE

- Preheat a smoker an hour prior to smoking.
- Use charcoal Cherry woods for smoking.
- Soak the Cherry wood chips before using

METHOD

1. Rub the chicken wings with garlic powder, smoked paprika, kosher salt, cayenne pepper, onion powder, and pepper.
2. Wrap the seasoned chicken wings with plastic wrap then let them sit for at least 2 hours. Refrigerate the chicken wings to keep them fresh.
3. After 2 hours, remove the seasoned chicken wings from the refrigerator then thaw at room temperature. Unwarp the seasoned chicken wings.
4. Light a fire in a ceramic smoker. Use charcoal and soaked Cherry wood chips to create smokes.
5. Set the rack in the smoker then insert ceramic plate and grate in it. Close the smoker.
6. Preheat the ceramic smoker to 325°F (163°C) and wait until it reaches the desired temperature.
7. Once the ceramic smoker is ready, arrange the seasoned chicken wings directly on the grate then smoke for an hour.
8. After an hour, take the chicken wings out of the ceramic smoker then arrange them in a disposable aluminum pan.
9. Combine honey with barbecue sauce and apple juice then mix well.
10. Baste the chicken wings with the honey mixture then return them back to the ceramic smoker. Maintain the temperature at 325°F (163°C).
11. Drizzle the remaining honey mixture then smoke the chicken wings for 2 hours more.
12. Once the internal temperature of the smoked chicken wings has reached 165°F (74°C), remove them from the ceramic smoker.
13. Transfer the smoked chicken wings to a serving dish then serve.
14. Enjoy!

Savory Smoked Chicken Crispy

(Total cook time 3 Hours 10 minutes)

Ingredients for 10 servings

- Boneless chicken breast (4-lbs., 1.8-kgs)

The Rub

- Salt – 2 tablespoons
- Pepper – 1 ½ teaspoons
- Paprika – 3 tablespoons
- Thyme – 2 tablespoons
- Garlic powder – 2 tablespoons
- Onion powder – 2 tablespoons
- Cayenne – 2 tablespoons

THE FIRE

- Preheat a smoker an hour prior to smoking.
- Use charcoal Cherry woods for smoking.
- Soak the Cherry wood chips before using

METHOD

1. Combine the rub ingredients—salt, pepper, paprika, thyme, garlic powder, onion powder, and cayenne in a bowl then stir well.
2. Rub the boneless chicken breast with the spice mixture then let it sit overnight.
3. Wrap with aluminum foil and store in the fridge to keep it fresh.
4. On the next day, place charcoal and soaked Cherry wood chips in a ceramic smoker then light a fire in it.
5. Set the rack in the smoker then insert ceramic plate and grate in it. Close the smoker.
6. Preheat the ceramic smoker to 300°F (148°C) and wait until it reaches the desired temperature.
7. Once the ceramic smoker is ready, remove the seasoned chicken from the fridge then place it on the grate.
8. Smoke the chicken for 2 hours then remove from the ceramic smoker.
9. Unwrap the chicken then return it back to the ceramic smoker. Place the chicken directly on the grate.
10. Smoke the chicken for an hour or until the internal temperature has reached 165°F (74°C).
11. Remove the smoked chicken from the ceramic smoker then transfer to a serving dish.
12. Serve and enjoy warm.

TURKEY

Chili Tomato Smoked Turkey Fritter

(TOTAL COOK TIME **15** MINUTES)

INGREDIENTS FOR **10** SERVINGS

- Ground turkey (4-lbs., 1.8-kgs)

THE SPICE

- Balsamic vinegar – ½ cup
- Dry red wine – ½ cup
- Salt – 1 teaspoon
- Pepper – 1 teaspoon
- Cayenne pepper – 2 teaspoons
- Diced tomato – ½ cup
- Red chili flakes – 3 tablespoons

The Glaze

- Butter – 3 tablespoons

The Fire

- Preheat a smoker an hour prior to smoking.
- Use charcoal and Apple woods for smoking.
- Soak the Apple wood chips for about an hour before using

Method

1. Combine ground turkey with the spice ingredients—balsamic vinegar, dry red wine, salt, pepper, cayenne pepper, diced tomato, and red chili flakes.
2. Using your hand, mix until the ingredients are well combined.
3. Divide the turkey mixture into 10 then shape into fritters forms.
4. Arrange the fritters on a tray then store in the fridge until set. It will take around 30 minutes.
5. Place charcoal and soaked Apple wood chips in a ceramic smoker then light a fire in it.
6. Set the rack in the smoker then insert ceramic plate and grate in it. Close the smoker.
7. Preheat the ceramic smoker to 400°F (204°C) and wait until it reaches the desired temperature.
8. Arrange the fritters on the ceramic smoker directly on the grate then smoke for 6 minutes.
9. After 6 minutes, open the ceramic smoker then baste the fritters with butter.
10. Flip the fritters then smoke again for another 6 minutes.
11. After the second 6 minutes, baste the fritter with butter again and smoke for 2 minutes.
12. Once it is done or the internal temperature of the turkey fritters has reached 165°F (74°C), remove from the ceramic smoker and arrange on a serving dish.
13. Serve and enjoy.

Onion Apple Smoked Whole Turkey

(TOTAL COOK TIME 3 HOURS 10 MINUTES)

Ingredients for 10 servings

- Whole Turkey (6-lbs., 2.7-kgs)

The Injection

- Butter – ½ cup

The Rub

- Lemon juice – ¼ cup
- Chili powder – 1 ½ tablespoons
- Paprika – 1 ½ tablespoons
- Black pepper – 1 tablespoon
- Onion powder – ¾ tablespoon
- Garlic powder – ¾ tablespoon
- Cayenne pepper – 1 teaspoon

THE FILLING

- Fresh apples – 2
- Chopped onion – 1 cup

THE FIRE

- Preheat a smoker an hour prior to smoking.
- Use charcoal and Apple woods for smoking.
- Soak the Apple wood chips for about an hour before using

METHOD

1. Drizzle lemon juice over the turkey then set aside.
2. Melt butter over low heat then let it cool.
3. Fill an injector with the melted butter then inject the turkey at several places.
4. Combine the rub ingredients—chili powder, paprika, black pepper, onion powder, garlic powder, and cayenne pepper in a bowl. Stir well.
5. Sprinkle the rub mixture all over the turkey and fill the turkey cavity with chopped apple and onion. Set aside.
6. Add charcoal and soaked Apple wood chips to the ceramic smoker then light a fire in it.
7. Set the rack in the smoker then insert a ceramic plate and a grate in it.
8. Preheat the ceramic smoker to 325°F (163°C) and wait until it reaches the desired temperature.
9. Place the seasoned turkey in the ceramic smoker then smoke for 2 hours and a half.
10. Check the internal temperature of the turkey and once it reaches 165°F (74°C), take the turkey out of the ceramic smoker.
11. Quickly wrap the smoked turkey with aluminum foil then let it rest for 30 minutes.
12. After 30 minutes, unwrap the smoked turkey then cut into pieces.
13. Serve and enjoy.

Smoked Juicy Turkey Drumsticks

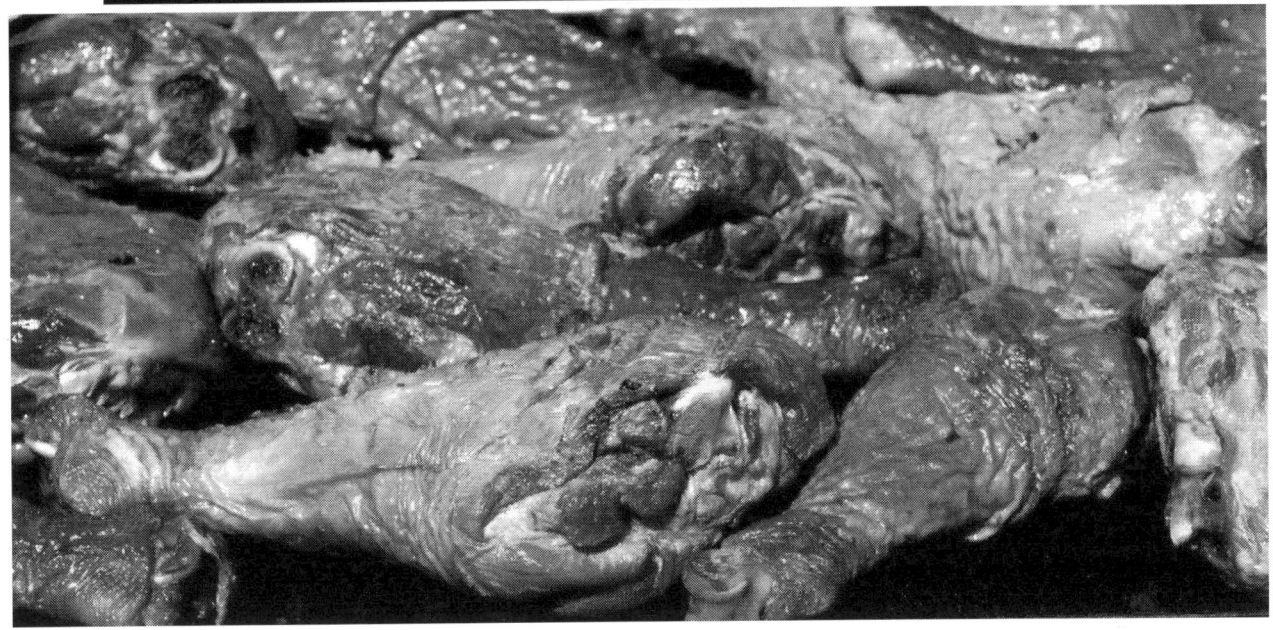

(Total cook time 3 hours 40 minutes)

Ingredients for 10 servings

- Turkey drumsticks (2-lbs., 0.9-kgs)

The Spice

- Water, room temperature – 2 cups
- Coarse salt – 3 tablespoons
- Brown sugar – ½ cup

The Fire

- Preheat a smoker an hour prior to smoking.
- Use charcoal and Apple woods for smoking.
- Soak the Apple wood chips for about an hour before using

Method

1. Pour water into a zipper-lock plastic bag then add salt and brown sugar to it. Stir well.
2. Put the turkey drumsticks in the zipper-lock plastic bag then shake until the turkey drums are seasoned.
3. Let the turkey legs sit overnight and store in the refrigerator to keep them fresh.
4. On the next day, remove the seasoned turkey drumsticks from the refrigerator.
5. Wash and rinse the turkey legs to avoid them becoming too salty. Pat them dry.
6. Place charcoal and soaked Apple wood chips in the ceramic smoker and light a fire in it.
7. Set the rack in the ceramic smoker and insert a ceramic plate and a grate in it.
8. Preheat the ceramic smoker to 325°F (163°C) and wait until it reaches the desired temperature.
9. Place a water pan on the ceramic plate and arrange the seasoned turkey drumsticks directly on the grate.
10. Smoke the turkey drumsticks for an hour and a half then reduce the temperature to 300°F (148°C).
11. Continue smoke the turkey drumsticks for an hour or until the internal temperature has reached 145°F (63°C).
12. Remove the smoked turkey drumsticks from the ceramic smoker and place on a serving dish.
13. Serve and enjoy.

GAME

SMOKED VENISON IN BACON BLANKET

(TOTAL COOK TIME 15 MINUTES)

INGREDIENTS FOR 10 SERVINGS

- Boneless venison (3-lbs., 1.4-kgs)
- Bacon (1-lb., 0.4-kgs

THE RUB

- Salt – 2 teaspoons
- Black pepper – 2 teaspoons
- Sweet paprika – 2 tablespoons

- Brown sugar – 1 ½ tablespoons
- White sugar – 1 tablespoon
- Thyme – 1 ½ tablespoon
- Garlic powder – 1 tablespoon
- Onion powder – 1 tablespoon
- Cayenne pepper – 1 teaspoon

THE FIRE

- Preheat a smoker an hour prior to smoking.
- Use charcoal and Pecan woods for smoking.
- Soak the Pecan wood chips for about an hour before using

METHOD

1. Combine the rub ingredients—salt, black pepper, sweet paprika, brown sugar, white sugar, thyme, garlic powder, onion powder, and cayenne pepper in a bowl then mix well.
2. Rub the venison with the spice mixture then wrap it with bacon. Let it rest.
3. Prepare a ceramic smoker for indirect heat using charcoal and soaked Pecan wood chips then light a fire in it.
4. Preheat the ceramic smoker to 275°F (135°C) then place the bacon wrapped venison in the ceramic smoker.
5. Smoke the bacon wrapped venison for 4-5 hours or until the internal temperature has reached 165°CF (74°C).
6. Once it is done, remove the smoked venison from the ceramic smoker then quickly wrap the smoked venison with aluminum foil. Let it rest for 20 minutes to an hour.
7. Unwrap the smoked venison then cut into slices.
8. Serve and enjoy.

Smoked Cornish Hen with Apple Coating

(Total cook time 2 hours 10 minutes)

Ingredients for 10 servings

- Cornish hen (3-lbs., 1.4-kgs)

The Spice

- Salt – 1 teaspoon
- Garlic powder – 3 teaspoons
- Chili powder – 1 ½ teaspoons

THE GLAZE

- Apple juice – 1 ½ cups
- Vinegar – 1 ½ tablespoon
- Chili powder – 1 teaspoon

THE FIRE

- Preheat a smoker an hour prior to smoking.
- Use charcoal and Apple woods for smoking.
- Soak the Apple wood chips for about an hour before using.

METHOD

1. Cut the Cornish hen into halves lengthwise then rub it with salt, garlic powder, and chili powder.
2. Place charcoal and soaked Apple wood chips then light a fire in it.
3. Prepare a ceramic smoker for indirect heat and preheat it to 275°F (135°C).
4. Once the ceramic smoker is ready, place the seasoned Cornish hen directly in the smoker then smoke it for about 2 hours. Use the vent to control the temperature.
5. ~~Meanwhile, combine the glaze mixture in a bowl.~~
6. Pour Apple juice into a bowl then add vinegar and chili powder to the bowl. Mix well.
7. At the last 30 minutes of smoking, baste the Cornish hen with the glaze mixture then continue smoking.
8. Once the smoked Cornish hen has reached 165°F (74°C), remove it from the smoker and place on a serving dish.
9. Serve with smoked vegetables.

Smoked Quails Jalapeno

(Total cook time 1 hours 40 minutes)

Ingredients for 10 servings

- Quails (2-lbs., 0.9-kgs)
- Bacon (0.5-lb., 0.2-kg)

The Marinade

- Garlic powder – 2 teaspoons
- Oregano – 2 tablespoons
- Chopped parsley – 1 tablespoon
- Basil – 1 teaspoon
- Sugar – 1 teaspoon

- Salt – 1 teaspoon
- Black pepper – 1 teaspoon

THE FILLING

- Chopped onion – ½ cup
- Diced jalapeno – 3 tablespoons

THE FIRE

- Preheat a smoker an hour prior to smoking.
- Use charcoal and Apple woods for smoking.
- Soak the Apple wood chips for about an hour before using.

METHOD

1. Combine the marinade ingredients—garlic powder, onion powder, oregano, parsley, basil, sugar, salt, and black pepper in a container then set aside.
2. Fill each quail's cavity with onion and jalapeno then wrap it with bacon. Repeat with the remaining quails then place them in the container with the marinade mixture.
3. Rub the quails with the spice then marinate for at least an hour. To keep them fresh, store the quails in the refrigerator.
4. After an hour, remove the seasoned quails from the refrigerator and thaw at room temperature.
5. Light a fire in a ceramic smoker then preheat it to 325°F (163°C).
6. Once it reaches the desired temperature, place the quails directly on the grate.
7. Smoke the quails for an hour to an hour and a half or until the internal temperature has reached 165°F (74°C).
8. Remove the smoked quails from the ceramic smoker then place on a serving dish.
9. Serve and enjoy.

SAVORY SMOKED PHEASANT

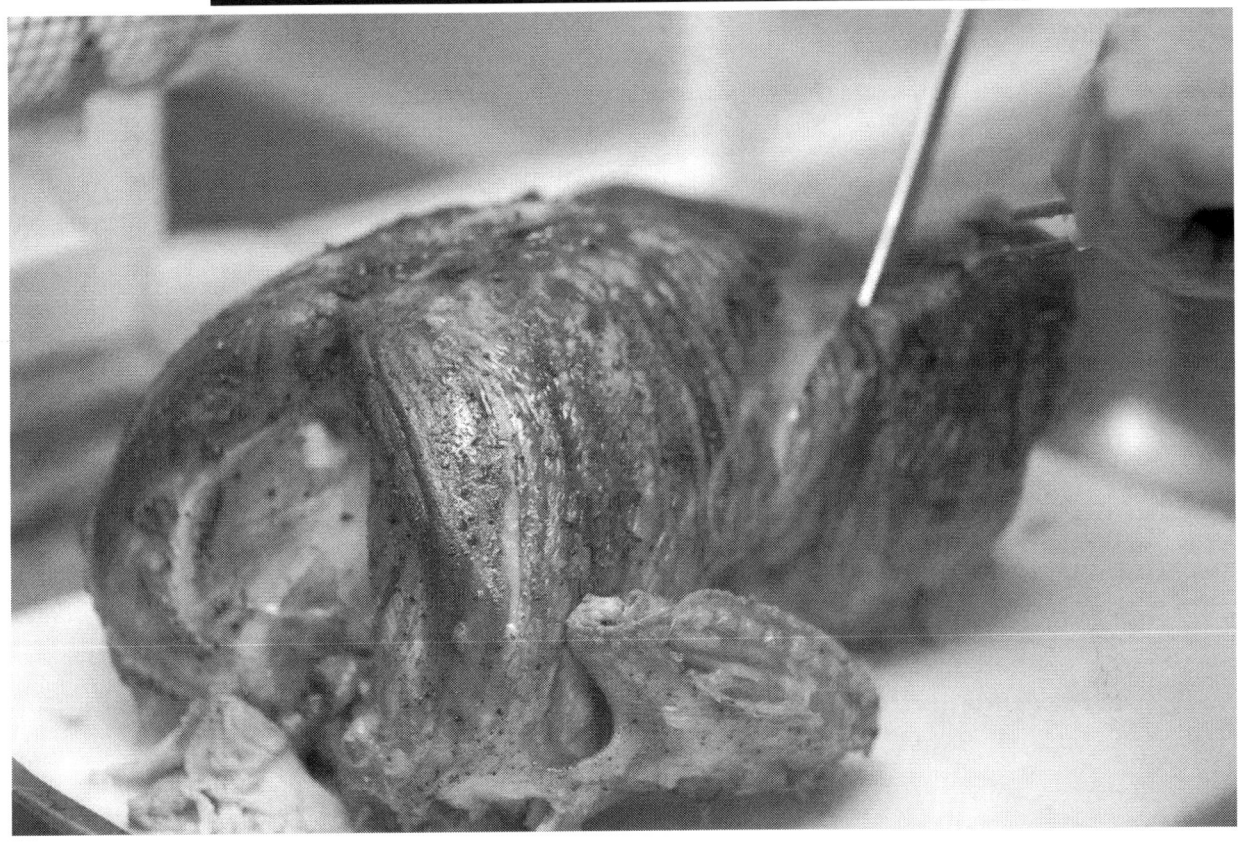

(TOTAL COOK TIME 3 HOURS 30 MINUTES)

INGREDIENTS FOR 10 SERVINGS

- Pheasant (2.5-lb, 1.1-kgs)

THE RUB

- Salt – 2 teaspoons
- Garlic powder – 2 teaspoons
- Onion powder – 2 teaspoons
- Chili powder – ½ teaspoon
- Black pepper – ½ teaspoon
- Cumin – ¼ teaspoon
- Cayenne pepper – ¼ teaspoon

THE FIRE

- Preheat a smoker an hour prior to smoking.
- Use charcoal and Apple woods for smoking.
- Soak the Apple wood chips for about an hour before using.

METHOD

1. Place the rub ingredients—salt, garlic powder, onion powder, chili powder, black pepper, cumin, and cayenne pepper in a bowl. Mix well.
2. Rub the pheasant with the spice mixture then marinate overnight. Store in the fridge to keep it fresh.
3. On the next day, remove the seasoned pheasant from the refrigerator then thaw at room temperature.
4. Place charcoal and soaked Apple wood chips in a ceramic smoker then light a fire in it.
5. Set the rack completed with the ceramic plate and the grate in the ceramic smoker then wait until the ceramic smoker has reached 250°F (121°C).
6. Once the smoker is ready, place the seasoned pheasant directly on the grate and smoke for 2 to 3 hours or until the internal temperature has reached 165°F (74°C).
7. Remove the smoked pheasant from the ceramic smoker and quickly wrap it with aluminum foil. Let it rest for 20 minutes.
8. Unwrap the smoked pheasant and place on a flat surface.
9. Cut it into pieces then serve.
10. Enjoy!

Information About Smoking Meat

What is the primary difference between Barbecuing a meat and Smoking it?

You might not believe it, but there are still people who think that the process of Barbecuing and Smoking are the same! So, this is something which you should know about before diving in deeper.

So, whenever you are going to use a traditional BBQ grill, you always put your meat directly on top of the heat source for a brief amount of time which eventually cooks up the meal. Smoking, on the other hand, will require you to combine the heat from your grill as well as the smoke to infuse a delicious smoky texture and flavor to your meat. Smoking usually takes much longer than traditional barbecuing. In most cases, it takes a minimum of 2 hours and a temperature of 100 -120 degrees for the smoke to be properly infused into the meat. Keep in mind that the time and temperature will obviously depend on the type of meat that you are using, and that is why it is suggested that you keep a meat thermometer handy to ensure that your meat is doing fine. Keep in mind that this method of barbecuing is also known as "Low and slow" smoking as well. With that cleared up, you should be aware that there are actually two different ways through which smoking is done.

THE CORE DIFFERENCE BETWEEN COLD AND HOT SMOKING

Depending on the type of grill that you are using, you might be able to get the option to go for a Hot Smoking Method or a Cold Smoking One. The primary fact about these three different cooking techniques which you should keep in mind are as follows:

- **Hot Smoking:** In this technique, the food will use both the heat on your grill and the smoke to prepare your food. This method is most suitable for items such as chicken, lamb, brisket etc.
- **Cold Smoking:** In this method, you are going to smoke your meat at a very low temperature such as 30 degree Celsius, making sure that it doesn't come into the direct contact with the heat. This is mostly used as a means to preserve meat and extend their life on the shelf.
- **Roasting Smoke:** This is also known as Smoke Baking. This process is essentially a combined form of both roasting and baking and can be performed in any type of smoker with a capacity of reaching temperatures above 82 degree Celsius.

THE DIFFERENT TYPES OF AVAILABLE SMOKERS

Essentially, what you should know is that right now in the market, you are going to get three different types of Smokers.

Charcoal Smoker

These types of smokers are hands down the best one for infusing the perfect Smoky flavor to your meat. But be warned, though, that these smokers are a little bit difficult to master as the method of regulating temperature is a little bit difficult when compared to normal Gas or Electric smokers.

Electric Smoker

After the charcoal smoker, next comes perhaps the simpler option, Electric Smokers. These are easy to use and plug and play type. All you need to do is just plug in, set the temperature and go about your daily life. The smoker will do the rest. However, keep in mind that the finishing smoky flavor won't be as intense as the Charcoal one.

Gas Smokers

Finally, comes the Gas Smokers. These have a fairly easy mechanism for temperature control and are powered usually by LP Gas. The drawback of these Smokers is that you are going to have to keep checking up on your Smoker every now and then to ensure that it has not run out of Gas.

THE DIFFERENT STYLES OF SMOKERS

The different styles of Smokers are essentially divided into the following.

Vertical (Bullet Style Using Charcoal)
These are usually low-cost solutions and are perfect for first-time smokers.

Vertical (Cabinet Style)
These Smokers come with a square shaped design with cabinets and drawers/trays for easy accessibility. These cookers also come with a water tray and a designated wood chips box as well.

Offset
These type of smokers have dedicated fireboxes that are attached to the side of the main grill. The smoke and heat required for these are generated from the firebox itself which is then passed through the main chamber and out through a nicely placed chimney.

Kamado Joe
And finally, we have the Kamado Joe which is ceramic smokers are largely regarded as being the "Jack Of All Trades".

These smokers can be used as low and slow smokers, grills, hi or low-temperature ovens and so on.

They have a very thick ceramic wall which allows it to hold heat better than any other type of smoker out there, requiring only a little amount of charcoal.

These are easy to use with better insulation and are more efficient when it comes to fuel control.

THE DIFFERENT TYPES OF WOOD AND THEIR BENEFITS

The Different Types Of Wood	Suitable For
Hickory	Wild game, chicken, pork, cheeses, beef
Pecan	Chicken, pork, lamb, cheeses, fish.
Mesquite	Beef and vegetables
Alder	Swordfish, Salmon, Sturgeon and other types of fishes. Works well with pork and chicken too.
Oak	Beef or briskets
Maple	Vegetable, ham or poultry
Cherry	Game birds, poultry or pork
Apple	Game birds, poultry, beef
Peach	Game birds, poultry or pork
Grape Vines	Beef, chicken or turkey
Wine Barrel Chips	Turkey, beef, chicken or cheeses
Seaweed	Lobster, mussels, crab, shrimp etc.
Herbs or Spices such as rosemary, bay leaves, mint, lemon peels, whole nutmeg etc.	Good for cheeses or vegetables and a small collection of light meats such as fillets or fish steaks.

THE DIFFERENT TYPES OF CHARCOAL

In General, there are essentially three different types of Charcoals. All of them are basically porous residues of black color that are made of carbon and ashes. However, the following are a little bit distinguishable due to their specific features.

- BBQ Briquettes: These are the ones that are made from a fine blend of charcoal and char.
- Charcoal Briquettes: These are created by compressing charcoal and are made from sawdust or wood products.
- Lump Charcoal: These are made directly from hardwood and are the most premium quality charcoals available. They are completely natural and are free from any form of the additive.

THE BASIC PREPARATIONS

- Always be prepared to spend the whole day and take as much time as possible to smoke your meat for maximum effect.
- Make sure to obtain the perfect Ribs/Meat for the meal which you are trying to smoke. Do a little bit of research if you need.
- I have already added a list of woods in this book, consult to that list and choose the perfect wood for your meal.
- Make sure to prepare the marinade for each of the meals properly. A great deal of the flavor comes from the rubbing.
- Keep a meat thermometer handy to get the internal temperature when needed.
- Use mittens or tongs to keep yourself safe
- Refrain yourself from using charcoal infused alongside starter fluid as it might bring a very unpleasant odor to your food
- Always make sure to start off with a small amount of wood and keep adding them as you cook.
- Don't be afraid to experiment with different types of wood for newer flavor and experiences.
- Always keep a notebook near you and note jot down whatever you are doing or learning and use them during the future session. This will help you to evolve and move forward.

THE CORE ELEMENTS OF SMOKING!

Smoking is a very indirect method of cooking that relies on a number of different factors to give you the most perfectly cooked meal that you are looking for. Each of these components is very important to the whole process as they all work together to create the meal of your dreams.

- **Time**: Unlike grilling or even Barbequing, smoking takes a really long time and requires a whole lot of patience. It takes time for the smoky flavor to slowly get infused into the meats. Jus to bring things into comparison, it takes an about 8 minutes to fully cook a steak through direct heating, while smoking (indirect heating) will take around 35-40 minutes.
- **Temperature:** When it comes to smoking, the temperature is affected by a lot of different factors that are not only limited to the wind, cold air temperatures but also the cooking wood's dryness. Some smokers work best with large fires that are controlled by the draw of a chimney and restricted airflow through the various vents of the cooking chamber and firebox. While other smokers tend to require smaller fire with fewer coals as well as a completely different combination of the vent and draw controls. However, most smokers are designed to work at temperatures as low as 180 degrees Fahrenheit to as high as 300 degrees Fahrenheit. But the recommend temperature usually falls between 250 degrees Fahrenheit and 275 degrees Fahrenheit.
- **Airflow:** The level of air to which the fire is exposed to greatly determines how your fire will burn and how quickly it will burn the fuel. For instance, if you restrict air flow into the firebox by closing up the available vents, then the fire will burn at a low temperature and vice versa. Typically in smokers, after lighting up the fire, the vents are opened to allow for maximum air flow and is then adjusted throughout the cooking process to make sure that optimum flame is achieved.
- **Insulation:** Insulation is also very important when it comes to smokers as it helps to easily manage the cooking process throughout the whole cooking session. A good insulation allows smokers to efficiently reach the desired temperature instead of waiting for hours upon hours!

CONCLUSION

I can't express how honored I am to think that you found my book interesting and informative enough to read it all through to the end. I thank you again for purchasing this book and I hope that you had as much fun reading it as I had writing it. I bid you farewell and encourage you to move forward and find your true Smoked Meat spirit!

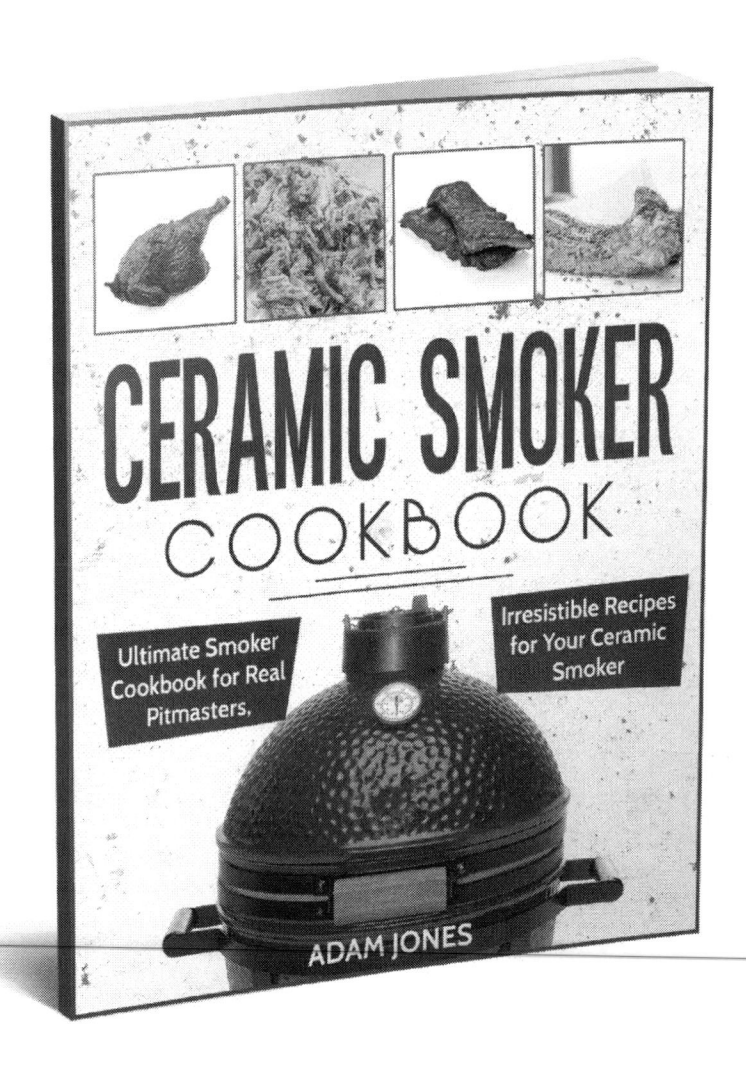

GET YOUR FREE GIFT

Suscribe to our Mail List and get your FREE copy of the book

'Smoking Meat: The Best 20 Recipes of Smoked Meat, Unique Recipes for Unique BBQ'

http://tiny.cc/smoke20

OTHER BOOKS BY ADAM JONES

https://www.amazon.com/dp/1720321590

https://www.amazon.com/dp/198756605X

SMOKING MEAT

Ultimate Smoker Cookbook for Real Pitmasters, Irresistible Recipes for Unique BBQ

ADAM JONES

https://www.amazon.com/dp/1548040959

https://www.amazon.com/dp/B07B3R82P4

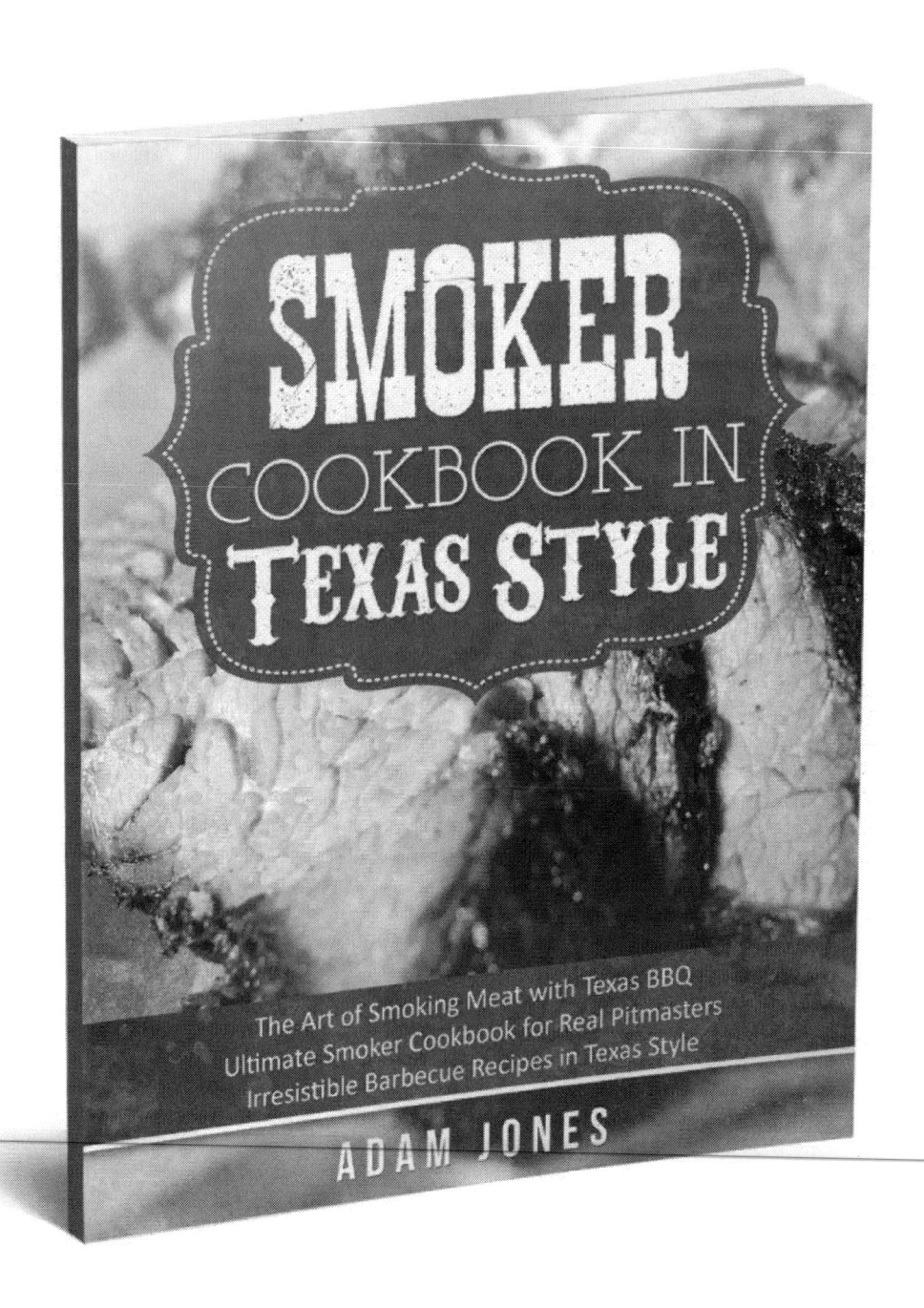

https://www.amazon.com/dp/B07B4YDKJ5

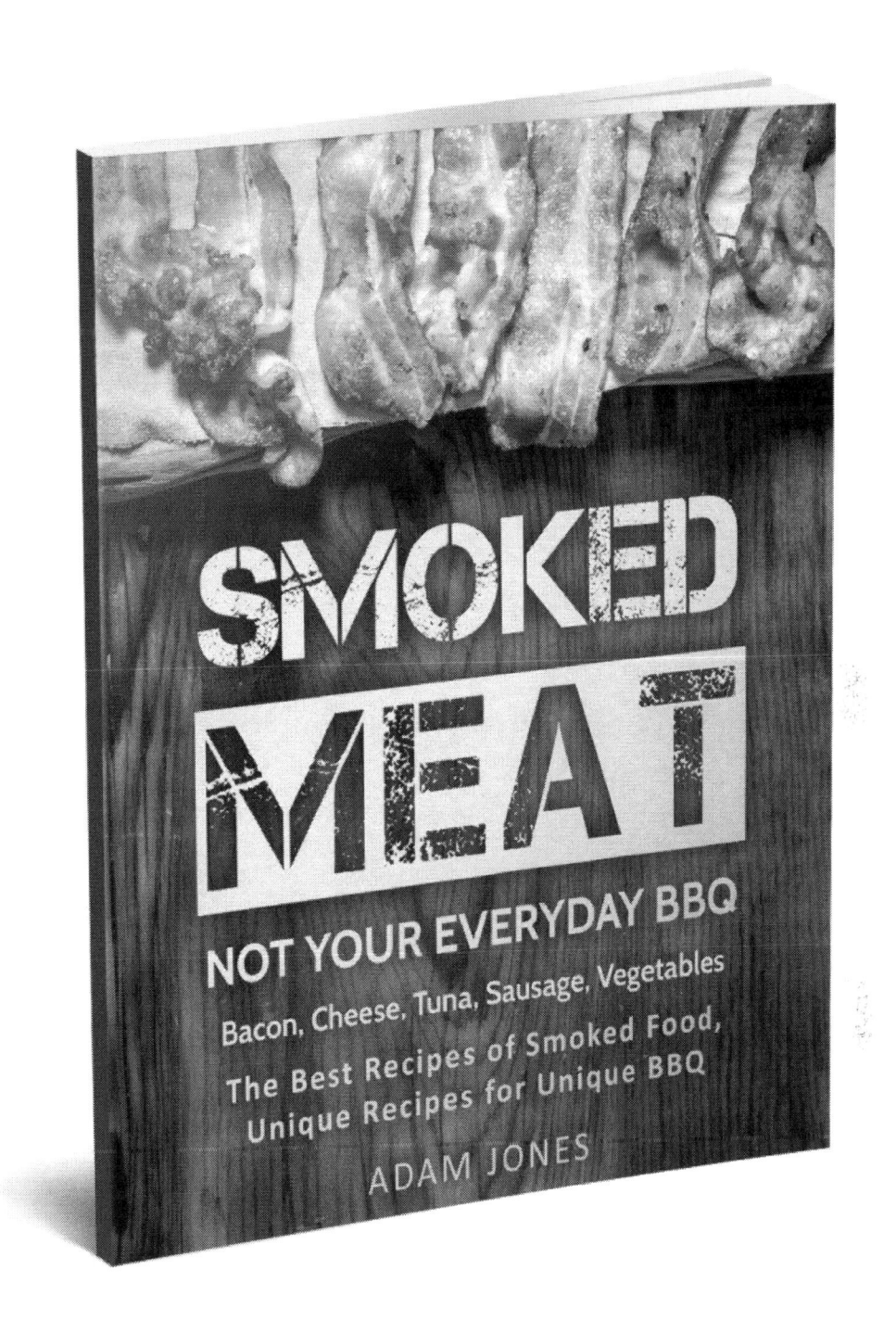

https://www.amazon.com/dp/1979559902

https://www.amazon.com/dp/1544791178

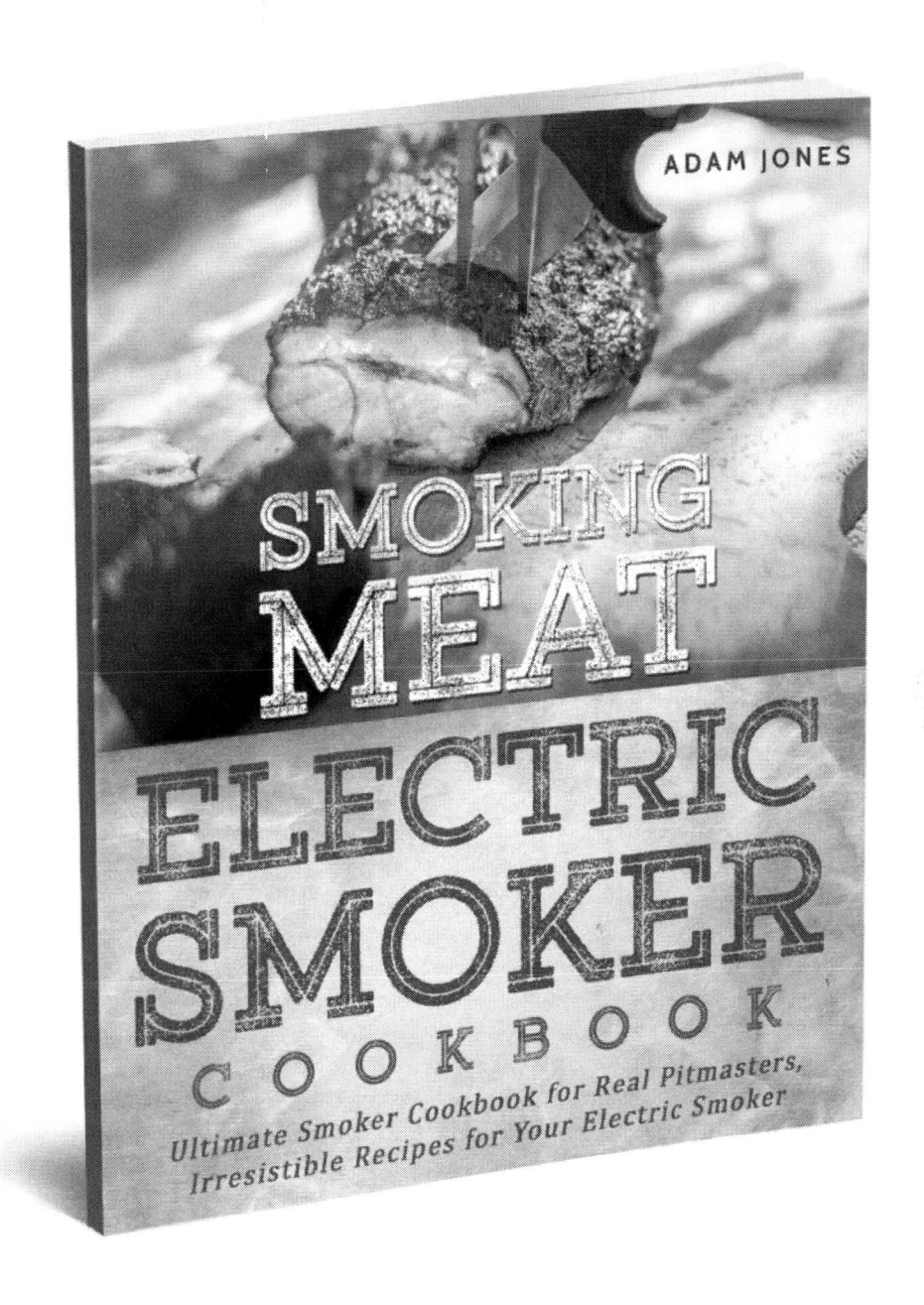

https://www.amazon.com/dp/1979811318

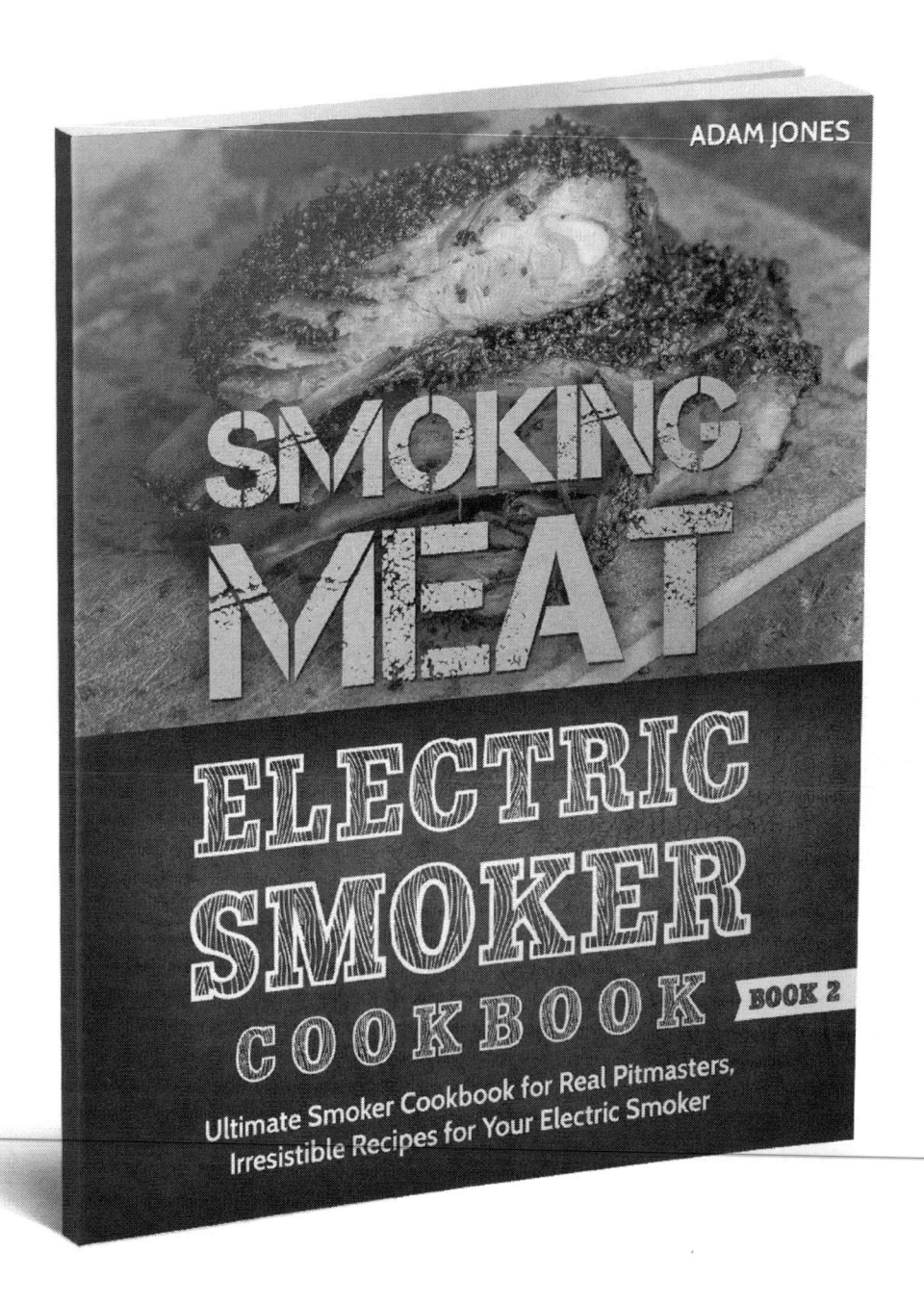

https://www.amazon.com/dp/1981617973

https://www.amazon.com/dp/1546605916

https://www.amazon.com/dp/1981940693

https://www.amazon.com/dp/1542597846

https://www.amazon.com/dp/1977677347

https://www.amazon.com/dp/154418199X

P.S. Thank you for reading this book. If you've enjoyed this book, please don't shy, drop me a line, leave a feedback or both on Amazon. I love reading reviews and your opinion is extremely important for me.

My Amazon page: www.amazon.com/author/adjones

©**Copyright 2018 by** <u>***Adam Jones***</u> - **All rights reserved.**

All rights Reserved. No part of this publication or the information in it may be quoted from or reproduced in any form by means such as printing, scanning, photocopying or otherwise without prior written permission of the copyright holder.

ISBN-13:
978-1720902850

ISBN-10:
1720902852

Disclaimer and Terms of Use:*The effort has been made to ensure that the information in this book is accurate and complete, however, the author and the publisher do not warrant the accuracy of the information, text, and graphics contained within the book due to the rapidly changing nature of science, research, known and unknown facts and the internet. The Author and the publisher do not hold any responsibility for errors, omissions or contrary interpretation of the subject matter herein. This book is presented solely for motivational and informational purposes only.*

Made in the USA
Monee, IL
13 March 2021